Nice Travel

2024

A Comprehensive Journey through History, Culture, and Splendor on the French Mediterranean Coast

Robert D. Richmond

TABLE OF CONTENTS

MAP OF NICE

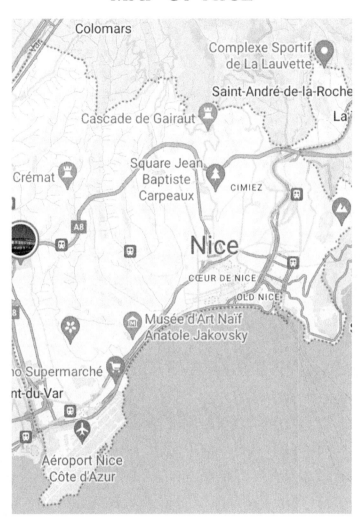

INTRODUCTION

In the heart of the French Riviera lies a city that whispers tales of elegance, beauty, and a timeless allure – Nice. Nestled between the cerulean embrace of the Mediterranean Sea and the sun-kissed hills of the Côte d'Azur, Nice stands as a canvas painted with strokes of history, culture, and captivating charm.

As you turn the pages of this travel guide, imagine strolling through the labyrinthine streets of Old Town, where the echoes of centuries past resonate with every step. Feel the gentle sea breeze along the iconic Promenade des Anglais, where the azure waters stretch as far as the eye can see, mirroring the limitless possibilities that await your exploration.

But beware, for Nice is more than just a picturesque postcard; it is a city that conceals secrets beneath its cobblestone alleys and behind the vibrant façades of its pastel-hued buildings. Unlock the mysteries of Castle Hill, where panoramic views will leave you breathless and where the shadows of ancient fortifications tell stories of conquests and triumphs.

Yet, this guide is not merely a collection of facts and figures – it is a key to unraveling the hidden gems and experiences that await the intrepid traveler. Discover the flavors of traditional Niçois cuisine, savor the magic of open-air markets, and indulge in the enchanting allure of the city's vibrant nightlife.

As the sun dips below the horizon, casting hues of pink and gold across the Mediterranean, the true spirit of Nice reveals itself – a city that beckons you to explore, savor, and lose yourself in its enchantment. But, dear reader, be prepared to surrender to the allure of Nice's secrets, for each page turned is a step deeper into the embrace of a city that refuses to be forgotten.

Join us on a journey beyond the ordinary, where every corner holds the promise of a new adventure. Let this guide be your passport to the captivating world of Nice, where history meets modernity and where the essence of the French Riviera awaits your discovery. Welcome to Nice – where the adventure begins, and the mystery never ends.

Brief History of Nice

Nice is a city with a long and illustrious history that dates back to antiquity. It is located on the French Riviera's radiant beaches. Founded in honor of Nike, the Greek goddess of victory, around 350 BCE, the Greek colony of Nikaia is where the city had its start. Over the ages, many nations and civilizations have sought after Nice due to its advantageous position along the Mediterranean.

In the second century BCE, the Romans conquered Nice after realizing its potential and left a lasting legacy of infrastructure and magnificent buildings. Cemenelum's remains, a Roman city that was once prosperous close to modern-day Nice, provide evidence of this period of imperial power.

Over the Middle Ages, the County of Provence, the House of Savoy, and the Angevin emperors all vied for control over Nice. These volatile periods saw the construction of the city's defenses, including the famous Castle Hill, which offered a commanding view of the surrounding landscapes and served as a defense against invaders.

Nice had significant changes throughout the 1800s. The city saw a transformation with the arrival of tourists and the

British nobility who came to enjoy the region's pleasant climate. Drawing tourists from all over Europe, the Promenade des Anglais is a promenade that runs across blue seas and has come to represent elegance and refinement.

During the Second World War, Nice saw both occupation and liberation, bringing its destiny into direct contact with historical events. The effects of the war were still felt, but Nice rose above the ruins to become the modern, multicultural sanctuary it is today.

Roman ruins, medieval walls, Belle Époque houses, and contemporary buildings are all examples of the city's varied architecture, which reflects its journey through time. Discover the layers of Nice's past by strolling around its quaint streets and piecing together its history. Nice's history is a tale of conquering, cultural interchange, and resiliency.

Fun facts and FAQs

Fun Facts

1. **The Greek Connection:** Nice has ancient roots, with its name derived from the Greek city of Nikaia. Founded by the Greeks around 350 BCE, the city's name pays homage to Nike, the goddess of victory.

2. **Sunshine Capital:** Nice is renowned for its exceptional climate, earning it the nickname "Nice la Belle" (Nice the Beautiful). The city boasts an average of 300 sunny days a year, making it a magnet for sun-seeking tourists.

3. **Promenade des Anglais:** The iconic Promenade des Anglais was initially built in the 19th century to accommodate English aristocrats who flocked to Nice for its mild climate. Today, it remains a scenic seaside boulevard perfect for strolls.

4. **Flower Power:** Nice hosts the famous Carnival of Nice, one of the world's largest and most colorful carnivals. The event features vibrant parades, intricate flower battles, and elaborate floats, attracting visitors from around the globe.

5. **Colline du Château:** While Castle Hill (Colline du Château) may no longer house a castle, it offers panoramic views of Nice and the Mediterranean. The journey to the top is worth the effort, with waterfalls, ruins, and lush greenery along the way.

6. **Cuisine Niçoise:** Nice is a culinary paradise, offering a unique blend of French and Mediterranean flavors. Don't miss out on local specialties such as Socca (chickpea pancake) and Salade Niçoise.

7. **Artistic Legacy:** The city has inspired renowned artists, including Henri Matisse and Marc Chagall. Both artists have museums dedicated to their works in Nice, showcasing the profound influence the city had on their creativity.

8. **Blue Waters:** The vivid azure color of the Mediterranean Sea along Nice's coastline is not just a postcard fantasy. The stunning blue hues are a testament to the region's pristine waters, inviting locals and visitors alike to indulge in beachside relaxation.

9. **Nice Jazz Festival:** For music enthusiasts, the annual Nice Jazz Festival is a must-attend event. Dating back to 1948, it is one of the oldest jazz festivals in the world, drawing top-notch performers and jazz fans from across the globe.

10. **Film Festival Connections:** Nice has played a role in the world of cinema, particularly through its proximity to Cannes. The city's stunning landscapes and vibrant atmosphere have made it a popular filming location for numerous movies, adding a touch of cinematic glamour to its allure.

FAQs

1. What is the best time to visit Nice?

Nice enjoys a Mediterranean climate, making it pleasant year-round. However, the best time to visit is during the spring (April to June) or fall (September to October) when the weather is mild and tourist crowds are thinner.

2. How do I get to Nice from the airport?

Nice Côte d'Azur Airport is well-connected. Options include taxis, buses, and the airport shuttle. Renting a car is also a convenient choice for exploring the French Riviera.

3. Which neighborhoods are recommended for accommodation?

Old Town (Vieux Nice) and the Promenade des Anglais are popular choices. Each neighborhood offers a unique atmosphere, with Old Town providing a historic charm and the Promenade offering stunning sea views.

4. Are English speakers widely understood in Nice?

While French is the official language, English is commonly spoken in tourist areas, hotels, and restaurants. Nevertheless, acquiring a set of fundamental French expressions can elevate your overall experience.

5. What are the must-try dishes in Nice?

Niçois cuisine is a delight. Don't miss the famous Salade Niçoise, Socca (chickpea pancake), and Ratatouille. Explore local bakeries for pastries like Pissaladière and Tarte Tropezienne.

6. What are the top cultural attractions in Nice?

Explore the museums, including the Musée Matisse and Marc Chagall National Museum. Dive into the history of Old Town, visit Castle Hill for panoramic views, and stroll along the elegant Place Masséna.

7. Are there day trips from Nice worth taking?

Absolutely! Consider day trips to Monaco, Cannes, Antibes, and the picturesque hilltop village of Eze for a diverse experience of the French Riviera.

8. How is the public transportation system in Nice?

Nice boasts an effective public transit network encompassing buses and trams. A regional train network connects Nice to nearby towns and cities, providing an easy way to explore the region.

9. What are some outdoor activities in Nice?

Enjoy outdoor adventures such as hiking in the surrounding hills, water sports on the Mediterranean, or cycling along the scenic routes in and around the city.

10. Do annual occasions or festivals take place in Nice?

Nice hosts numerous events, including the renowned Nice Carnival, the Jazz à Juan Festival, and vibrant Bastille Day celebrations. Check the calendar for local festivities during your visit.

Why Visit Nice?

Traveling to Nice is like walking into a brightly colored painting where the Mediterranean's hues come to life, and each cobblestone has a story of timeless splendor. I feel obligated to tell the tale of a city that enchants the spirit and makes a lasting impression on the heart because I have personally experienced the Nice magic.

Imagine yourself walking down the sun-drenched Promenade des Anglais, with the Mediterranean's blue seas extending out in front of you indefinitely. The opening notes of a symphony that expands with every step are the warmth of the sun and the soft caress of the sea air. Explore Old Town's maze-like lanes, where the historically significant buildings narrate the story of a city that has accepted the past while transitioning smoothly into the future.

Nice is more than just a place to visit; it's an opportunity to fully experience the charms of the French Riviera. You can smell the delicious scent of traditional Niçois food wafting through the air, beckoning you to revel in the region's culinary riches and experience the flavors of Ratatouille. With its expansive views, Castle Hill serves as a contemplative spot where the contemporary and historical aspects of the city come together to create a stunning vista.

However, there is something more than picture-perfect scenery—an atmosphere and enchantment that seeps into your soul. It's the cheerful marketplaces, the sound of music on hot summer evenings, and the laughing that fills the quaint squares. Nice is a call to embrace the unexpected and revel in life's little joys.

So, my dear traveler, come to Nice as a seeker of magic as much as a guest. Allow the embrace of the city to envelop you, and immerse yourself in an enduring tale that is just waiting to be written in time to match your footsteps down the alluring French Riviera coast.

Geography of Nice

Nice, which is located on the sun-drenched French Riviera, has a terrain that combines the Mediterranean Sea's blue vastness with its undulating hills and colorful metropolitan surroundings. Nestled between the sea and the Mercantour National Park, Nice, in the Provence-Alpes-Côte d'Azur area, is a picture of unspoiled beauty.

The famous Promenade des Anglais, a gorgeous length of the Baie des Anges where palm-lined boulevards beckon strolls and provide an unhindered view of the sea's glittering horizon, is the focal point of the city. While the famous beaches of Nice provide a sun-seekers paradise to the west, the port area beckons to the east with its vibrant vitality.

As one travels inward, the scenery changes to the steep Côte d'Azur, with Castle Hill, also known as Colline du Château, serving as a notable landmark that provides expansive views over the city and its environs. Mont Boron and Cimiez, two communities with unique charms and personalities, are set against the rolling hills as a background.

Not only has a background, the city's topography affected everything from its temperature to the outdoor activities it provides. It is an essential aspect of the city's character. Nice's geography is a canvas upon which a multitude of experiences are painted, inviting visitors to immerse themselves in the distinctive and diverse landscapes that define this jewel of the French Riviera, whether they are strolling through the verdant hillsides or sunbathing on the pebbled shores.

PLANNING YOUR TRIP

Visa and Entry Requirements

Do you need a visa?

Whether you need a visa depends on your nationality. Most visitors from countries within the Schengen Area, including the US, Canada, Australia, and New Zealand, can enjoy visa-free entry for up to 90 days within 180 days.

If you need a visa

- **Types of visas:** Different visa types cater to various purposes, such as tourism, business, study, or work. Identify the one that aligns with your travel goals.

- **Application process:** Apply for your visa well in advance at the nearest French embassy or consulate in your home country. The process typically involves submitting documents like your passport, application form, proof of financial means, and travel insurance.

- **Visa fees:** Visa fees vary depending on your nationality and visa type. Check the French embassy or consulate website for the latest fee information.

General entry requirements for all visitors

- **Valid passport:** Your passport must be valid for at least three months beyond your intended stay in France.
- **Proof of accommodation:** Show confirmation of your hotel booking, rental agreement, or invitation from a host.
- **Proof of financial means:** Demonstrate sufficient funds to cover your stay in France. This can be through bank statements, credit cards, or traveler's checks.
- **Proof of onward travel:** Show a confirmed return or onward travel ticket out of France.
- **Health insurance:** Ensure you have adequate health insurance coverage for your trip.

Best Time to visit

The best time to visit Nice really depends on what you're looking for in your trip! Here is an analysis outlining the advantages and disadvantages of each season:

Summer (June-August)

- **Pros:** Hot and sunny weather, perfect for swimming and sunbathing (average highs in the low 80s F), lively atmosphere with lots of festivals and events, long days with up to 14 hours of sunshine.

- **Cons:** Crowded and expensive, beaches can be packed, accommodation can be hard to find and expensive.

Shoulder Seasons (April-May & September-October)

- **Pros:** Pleasant weather with average highs in the 60s and 70s F, fewer crowds than in summer, lower prices, still plenty of sunshine, and opportunity for outdoor activities.

- **Cons:** The Sea may be too cool for swimming for some people, and some businesses may have shorter hours or be closed.

Winter (November-March)

- **Pros:** Mild weather with average highs in the 50s F, the cheapest time to visit, fewer crowds, and a chance to see the Christmas markets.

- **Cons:** Some attractions may be closed, rainy days are more common, and the sea is too cold for swimming.

Here are some additional factors to consider:

- **Events:** If there's a specific event you want to attend, such as the Nice Carnival (February-March) or the Nice Jazz Festival (July), plan your trip around that.

- **Budget:** Prices are highest in summer and lowest in winter.

- **Interests:** If you're interested in outdoor activities like hiking or biking, spring and fall are the best times to go. If you're looking for a beach vacation, summer is the best choice.

Explore Nice: A 5-Day Itinerary

DAY 1: A Stroll through Old Town and Castle Hill Views

- **MORNING:** Begin your exploration of Nice with a delightful breakfast at Côté Lounge, offering a serene start to the day. Afterward, immerse yourself in the charming ambiance of Nice Old Town (Vieux Nice), where you can wander through narrow streets and visit the vibrant Cours Saleya Flower Market (Marché aux Fleurs Cours Saleya). Take in the history at the St. Nicholas Cathedral (Cathédrale Saint-Nicolas) and enjoy the panoramic views from the top of Castle Hill (Colline du Château).

- **AFTERNOON:** For lunch, head to La Havane for a taste of their Cuban-inspired cuisine. Post-lunch, take a leisurely walk along the famous Promenade des Anglais, enjoying the sea breeze and the beautiful azure waters. Continue to the Massena Square (Place Masséna), the vibrant heart of the city, and explore the nearby Massena Art & History

Museum (Musée Masséna) to delve into the local history and art.

- **EVENING:** As the day winds down, savor a sophisticated dinner at La Terrasse du Plaza, offering a refined atmosphere and exquisite dishes. Afterward, enjoy a leisurely evening walk along the Quai des États-Unis, soaking in the evening lights and the relaxed ambiance of the French Riviera.

DAY 2: Perfume and Palatial Gardens

- **MORNING:** Start your day with a sumptuous breakfast at Le Blue Whales, known for its fresh and diverse offerings. After breakfast, embark on a short drive to the picturesque village of Èze and visit the Exotic Garden of Èze (Jardin Exotique d'Èze). Explore the garden's unique plant species and enjoy a panoramic view of the Mediterranean.

- **AFTERNOON:** For lunch, head to El Merkado to experience their fusion cuisine in a vibrant setting. Post-lunch, continue your olfactory journey with a visit to the Molinard Perfumery (Maison Molinard) in Grasse, where you can learn about the art of perfume making and even create your signature scent.

- **EVENING:** Dine at Bistro Apéro, a cozy restaurant offering a selection of small plates and a relaxed atmosphere. After dinner, take a stroll through the gardens of Villa Ephrussi de Rothschild, enjoying the beautiful architecture and the serene evening ambiance.

DAY 3: Art and Cultural Immersion

- **MORNING:** Enjoy a delightful breakfast at Moon Bar, known for its panoramic views and a great start to the day. After breakfast, visit the Marc Chagall National Museum (Musée National Marc Chagall) to admire the works of the renowned artist. Continue to the Matisse Museum (Musée Matisse) to explore the masterpieces in a tranquil setting.

- **AFTERNOON:** For lunch, indulge in the flavors of Warehouse Restaurant Club, offering a diverse menu in a stylish industrial-chic setting. Post-lunch, take a scenic drive to the Maeght Foundation (Fondation Maeght) in Saint-Paul-de-Vence, where you can immerse yourself in a world of modern and contemporary art, both indoors and in the beautiful outdoor spaces.

- **EVENING:** Dine at L'EssenCiel panoramic restaurant, where you can enjoy not only a delectable meal but also breathtaking views of the city. After dinner, experience the vibrant nightlife of Nice at Movida, a popular spot for drinks and music.

DAY 4: Scenic Villages and Monastic Serenity

- **MORNING:** Start your day with a hearty breakfast at Seven Blue Bar, energizing you for the day ahead. Then, set out to explore the medieval village of Tourrettes-sur-Loup, known for its charming streets and artisan shops. Take your time to soak in the Provencal atmosphere before heading to the Cimiez Monastery (Monastere de Cimiez) to enjoy the peaceful surroundings and visit the nearby Nice Museum of Asian Arts (Musée des Arts Asiatiques).

- **AFTERNOON:** For lunch, enjoy the casual elegance of Van Diemen's, offering a menu inspired by local and international flavors. Afterward, take a scenic drive to the Villefranche-sur-Mer and explore the colorful old town and the Villefranche Cruise Port (Port de la Santé). If time allows, you can also visit the nearby Mt. Boron (Mont Boron) for panoramic views of the coast.

- **EVENING:** Dine at Snug And Cellar, a hidden gem known for its cozy atmosphere and a menu featuring seasonal and local ingredients. After dinner, take a leisurely evening walk in the gardens of Villa Kerylos, an exquisite recreation of an ancient Greek dwelling, offering a serene end to the day.

DAY 5: Riviera Panoramas and Historic Estates

- **MORNING:** Begin your final day with a breakfast at O'Neill's Pub, where you can enjoy a hearty Irish start. After breakfast, take a scenic drive along the Nice Corniche Roads (Les Trois Corniches), exploring the stunning coastal views and making a stop at the Fort du Mont Alban to appreciate the historical significance and the panoramic vistas.

- **AFTERNOON:** For lunch, visit FOAM Nice, Port Lympia Bar à Bière - Craft Beer Bars for a unique culinary experience paired with a selection of craft beers. Post-lunch, continue your journey to the Chateau de Cremat, where you can enjoy a guided tour of the vineyards and a tasting of the local wines in a beautiful setting.

- **EVENING:** Conclude your trip with a memorable dinner at Ma Nolan's Irish Pub, Nice Port, known for its lively atmosphere and a menu featuring classic pub fare with a twist. After dinner, enjoy the vibrant nightlife of Nice at Castellane, exploring the bars and entertainment venues in the area.

Tips to Save Money

Nice, nestled on the French Riviera, offers sun, culture, and charm galore – but it can also feel expensive. However, with a little planning and savvy, you can experience the best of Nice without breaking the bank. Here are some tips to help you save money:

Accommodation

- **Travel Off-Season:** Avoid peak season (July-August) and visit during the shoulder months (May-

June, September-October) for lower prices on flights and accommodations.

- **Consider Alternative Stays:** Explore hostels, guesthouses, or Airbnb's in neighborhoods outside the main tourist center.
- **Stay outside the City:** Consider towns like Cagnes-sur-Mer or Menton for cheaper options, with easy access to Nice by train or bus.

Food and Drinks

- **Self-Catering:** Skip expensive restaurants and opt for grocery shopping at local markets or supermarkets. Enjoy picnics in parks, beaches, or your rental balcony.
- **Lunchtime Deals:** Many restaurants offer affordable lunch menus (formules du midi) with good portions.
- **Happy Hour:** Take advantage of happy hour deals for discounted drinks and snacks at bars and cafes.
- **Explore Local Markets:** Sample delicious and affordable street food at vibrant markets like Cours Saleya in the Old Town.

Activities and Transportation

- **Free Fun:** Nice offers plenty of free things to do, from strolling the scenic Promenade des Anglais to exploring the Old Town with its colorful houses and narrow streets. Visit museums on free admission days or participate in free cultural events.

- **Nice Museums Pass:** Consider the Nice Museums Pass for discounted or free entry to several museums and galleries.

- **French Riviera Pass:** If you plan on visiting multiple attractions, the French Riviera Pass offers free entry to various museums and landmarks and discounts on public transportation and excursions.

- **Walk and Bike:** Nice, it is compact and walkable. Rent a bike for a fun and affordable way to explore the city and surrounding areas.

- **Public Transportation:** Utilize the efficient bus and tram network for affordable travel around Nice.

- **Day Trips:** Consider budget-friendly day trips to nearby towns like Antibes, Menton, or Villefranche-sur-Mer, accessible by train or bus.

Additional Tips

- **Book in Advance:** Secure flights and accommodations early for better deals, especially during peak season.
- **Travel Discounts:** Check for student discounts or senior rates on attractions and transportation.
- **Plan Your Activities:** Prioritize your must-sees and research free or discounted options before you go.
- **Pack Light:** Avoid baggage fees by packing light and taking advantage of self-service laundromats if needed.

Remember, flexibility is key! Embrace the local experience, explore off-the-beaten-path corners, and be open to discoveries. With these tips and a bit of resourcefulness, you can enjoy the best of Nice without burning a hole in your pocket.

GETTING TO NICE

How to Get There

From North America

Getting to Nice, France, from North America is possible through various modes of transportation, each with its advantages and disadvantages. Here's a breakdown of the different options:

Flights

- **Direct flights:** Several airlines offer direct flights from major North American cities like New York, Chicago, Toronto, Atlanta, and Los Angeles to Nice Côte d'Azur Airport (NCE). Flight time is typically around 10-12 hours. Popular airlines include Air France, American Airlines, Delta Air Lines, United Airlines, and Air Canada.

- **Connecting flights:** If direct flights are unavailable or too expensive, you can consider connecting flights with one or two layovers in European cities like Amsterdam, Paris, London, or Frankfurt. This option might take longer (up to 15-20 hours) but could be more affordable, especially with budget airlines like Lufthansa, KLM, Iberia, or Norwegian Air.

Cruise

- **Transatlantic cruises:** Several major cruise lines offer transatlantic cruises from North American cities like New York, Miami, or Fort Lauderdale to European ports like Barcelona or Civitavecchia (Rome), from where you can take a train or regional flight to Nice. This option is a leisurely way to travel, often with all-inclusive packages and onboard entertainment, but it takes significantly longer (up to 10-14 days).

Train

- **No direct train routes:** Unfortunately, there's no direct train connection between North America and Nice. However, you could take a train from a major North American city to New York or Montreal, then fly to a European city with good train connections to Nice, like Paris or Zurich. This option is time-consuming (up to 20-30 hours) but could be scenic and comfortable, especially if you choose high-speed trains.

Other options

- **Ferry:** A less common option is to take a ferry from Morocco or Algeria to southern France, then travel to Nice by train or bus. This is a budget-friendly option but can be time-consuming and have limited schedules.

Here are some additional factors to consider when choosing your mode of transportation:

- **Budget:** Flights are generally the fastest option but can be expensive, especially during peak season. Cruises and trains offer more affordable options but take longer.

- **Time:** If you're short on time, direct flights are the best option. If you have more time, you can consider cruises or trains for a more leisurely experience.

- **Comfort:** Consider your preferred level of comfort when choosing your mode of transportation. Some people prefer the spaciousness and amenities of cruise ships, while others prefer the speed and convenience of airplanes.

- **Personal preferences:** Ultimately, the best way to get to Nice from North America is the one that best suits your individual needs and preferences.

From Asia

By plane

- This is the quickest and most convenient option, but also the most expensive. Many airlines offer flights from major Asian cities to Nice, with layovers in the Middle East or Europe. Some possible flight companies include Emirates, Qatar Airways, Turkish Airlines, Lufthansa, and Air France.
- Flying time from most Asian cities to Nice will be between 12 and 16 hours, with one or two layovers.
- The cost of a flight from Asia to Nice will vary depending on the airline, the time of year you travel, and whether you book in advance. However, you can expect to pay between $500 and $2,000 for a round-trip ticket.

By train

- Taking the train from Asia to Nice is a more adventurous and scenic option, but it is also much slower than flying. There is no direct train route from Asia to Nice, so you will need to take a series of trains with connections in Europe. Some possible routes include taking the Trans-Siberian Railway from Moscow to Paris and then connecting to Nice by TGV.

- Train travel from Asia to Nice can take up to two weeks or more and will require multiple train changes.
- The cost of train travel from Asia to Nice will vary depending on the route you take and the type of ticket you purchase. However, you can expect to pay between $500 and $1,500 for a one-way ticket.

By bus

- Taking the bus from Asia to Nice is the cheapest option, but it is also the slowest. There are a few companies that offer bus routes from major Asian cities to Europe, with stops in Nice. One company that offers this service is Ecolines.
- Bus travel from Asia to Nice can take up to three weeks or more and will require multiple bus changes.

- The cost of bus travel from Asia to Nice will vary depending on the route you take and the type of ticket you purchase. Anticipate a cost ranging from $200 to $500 for a single-way ticket.

Once you have arrived in Nice, there are a few different ways to get around the city:

- **By public transportation:** Nice has a well-developed public transportation system, including buses, trams, and a light rail line. Tickets can be purchased from vending machines at bus stops and tram stations.
- **By bike:** Nice is a great city to explore by bike. There are many bike rental shops in the city, and there are also a number of designated bike lanes.
- **On foot:** The best way to see Nice is on foot. The city is relatively small and walkable, and there are many interesting sights to see along the way.

From South America

By Air

- **Nonstop flights:** The fastest way to get to Nice from major South American cities like São Paulo, Rio de Janeiro, or Buenos Aires is with a nonstop flight. Airlines offering this service include Air France, KLM, LATAM Airlines, and Aerolíneas Argentinas. Flight time typically ranges from 12 to 15 hours.

- **Flights with one stopover:** This option offers more flexibility and potentially lower fares, especially if you're willing to consider less popular airlines. Some good options include flying with Iberia via Madrid, Turkish Airlines via Istanbul, or Ethiopian Airlines via Addis Ababa.

By Sea

- **Transatlantic cruises:** If you're looking for a truly luxurious and leisurely travel experience, consider taking a transatlantic cruise from South America to Europe. Several major cruise lines, such as MSC Cruises and Costa Cruises, offer itineraries that include stops in Nice. The journey typically takes two to three weeks, with plenty of time to relax, enjoy onboard amenities, and explore exciting ports along the way.

By Land and Sea

- **Combine flights and ferries:** For a more adventurous option, you could fly from South America to a European city like Lisbon or Barcelona and then take a ferry across the Mediterranean Sea to Nice. This gives you the chance to experience different cultures and landscapes along the way.

From Africa

By Plane: This is the quickest and most convenient option, with several airlines offering flights from major African cities to Nice. Here are some of the airlines that fly to Nice from Africa:

- **Air France:** Flies from Johannesburg, Cape Town, and Durban in South Africa, as well as from Casablanca in Morocco.
- **Emirates:** Offers flights from Johannesburg, Cape Town, and Durban in South Africa, as well as from Accra in Ghana, Lagos in Nigeria, and Nairobi in Kenya.
- **Royal Air Maroc:** Flies from Casablanca, Morocco to Nice.

- **Ethiopian Airlines:** Offers flights from Addis Ababa, Ethiopia to Nice.
- **Tunisair:** Flies from Tunis, Tunisia, to Nice.

The flight time will vary depending on your origin city, but expect it to be between 11 and 15 hours for a direct flight. Prices can also vary depending on the airline, season, and how far in advance you book. You can find the best deals by using a flight comparison website or app.

Connecting Flights

If there are no direct flights from your city to Nice, you will need to take a connecting flight. This may involve flying to another European city, like Paris or Frankfurt, and then connecting to Nice. While this will add to your travel time, it can sometimes be cheaper than a direct flight.

Other Travel Options

While less common, you can also get to Nice from Africa by:

- **Ferry:** There are ferries from Morocco to Spain, from where you can take a train or bus to Nice. This is a more scenic option, but it will take much longer than flying.

- **Car:** If you're adventurous, you can drive from Africa to Nice. This is a long and challenging journey, but it can be a rewarding experience. However, keep in mind that you will need to obtain the necessary visas and permits, and you should be prepared for the challenging road conditions in some parts of Africa.

PRACTICAL TIPS FOR TRAVELERS

Transportation within the City

Nice offers a variety of convenient and affordable options for getting around the city, whether you're a local or a tourist. Here's a breakdown of your transportation options:

Public Transport

- **Buses & Tram:** The Lignes d'Azur network operates an extensive bus and tram system covering the city and beyond. A single ticket costs €1.50 and allows you to transfer between buses and trams within 74 minutes. Several ticket options are available, including multi-trip tickets, day passes, and 7-day passes.

- **Train:** The Nice-Ville station connects you to other cities along the French Riviera, like Cannes and Monaco, and further afield within France.

Eco-Friendly options

- **Biking:** Nice is a bike-friendly city with over 100km of dedicated cycle paths. You can rent bicycles from several companies, including

Vélobleu (the city's public bike-sharing program) and private shops.

- **Walking:** Exploring on foot is a great way to experience Nice's charm and soak in the sights. The city center is compact and walkable, and the beautiful Promenade des Anglais provides a scenic route along the coast.

Other options

- **Taxis:** Taxis are readily available throughout the city, though they can be expensive. Hail a cab on the roadside or contact a taxi service by phone.
- **Ride-sharing:** Apps like Uber are available in Nice and can be a convenient option for shorter trips.

Here are some additional tips for getting around Nice:

- **Download the Lignes d'Azur app:** This app provides real-time information on bus and tram schedules and locations.
- **Purchase a Nice Côte d'Azur Card:** This card offers discounts on public transport, museums, and other attractions.

- **Validate your ticket:** Remember to validate your ticket on buses and trams by stamping it at the machines upon entering.
- **Consider your needs:** For shorter trips, walking or cycling might be the most enjoyable option. If you're carrying luggage or traveling with a group, taking a taxi or using a ride-sharing app might be more convenient.

Safety Tips

While Nice is generally a safe city, like any tourist destination, it's always wise to be informed and take precautions. Here are some safety tips for your trip:

General

- **Be aware of your surroundings:** This is especially important in crowded areas like the Promenade des Anglais and Old Town. Keep an eye on your belongings and avoid distractions that could make you a target for pickpockets.
- **Keep valuables safe:** Leave important documents and large sums of cash in your hotel safe. Carry only what you need for the day, and consider using

a money belt or cross-body bag to secure your belongings.

- **Dress appropriately:** While bikinis and bare chests are acceptable on the beach, keep them covered up away from the shore. Respect local customs and dress modestly in restaurants, religious sites, and government buildings.
- **Learn basic French:** Knowing a few key phrases can help you communicate effectively and navigate the city more easily.
- **Download essential apps:** Install helpful apps like Google Translate, offline maps, and emergency contact information for the French Riviera.

Specific areas

- **Avoid certain areas:** While Nice is generally safe, some areas, like the Ariane and Moulins neighborhoods, have higher crime rates and should be avoided, especially at night.
- **Be cautious at night:** While walking around at night is generally safe, stick to well-lit areas and main streets. If you're alone, consider taking a taxi or Uber instead of walking long distances.

- **Be careful on public transportation:** Be aware of your belongings on trams and buses, as these are common locations for petty theft.

Beach safety

- **Don't leave valuables unattended:** The beaches are popular with pickpockets, so take only what you need and keep an eye on them at all times. It is advisable to store your valuable items at your hotel.
- **Beware of strong currents:** The Mediterranean Sea can be unpredictable, so pay attention to warning flags and signs. Swim between lifeguard flags and follow their instructions.
- **Protect yourself from the sun:** Use sunscreen with SPF 30 or higher, wear a hat and sunglasses, and stay hydrated, especially during the hottest parts of the day.

Additional tips

- **Purchase travel insurance:** This will provide financial protection in case of medical emergencies, lost luggage, or trip cancellations.

- **Register with your embassy:** Let your embassy or consulate know your travel plans so they can assist you in case of an emergency.
- **Learn about local scams:** Be aware of common scams targeting tourists, such as overcharging for taxis or pickpocketing distractions.

Wi-Fi and Connectivity

Free Wi-Fi

- **City of Nice:** The city provides free high-speed Wi-Fi in key areas like tram stops, the Promenade du Paillon Gardens, Place Massena, Place Garibaldi, Cours Saleya, the Palais du Justice, and around tourist offices. Look for the network named "Nice_FR."
- **Restaurants and Cafes:** Most establishments offer free Wi-Fi to customers. Just ask for the password!
- **Nice Côte d'Azur Airport:** Enjoy free, unlimited Wi-Fi throughout the airport with the network "NiceAirportFreeWifi."

Paid Wi-Fi

- **Hotels and apartments:** Most accommodations offer Wi-Fi as part of the stay. Check with your host for details.

- **Mobile data:** French mobile carriers like Orange, SFR, and Bouygues Telecom offer data plans for visitors. Consider purchasing a SIM card if you need extensive mobile internet access.

Connectivity Tips

- Download offline maps and essential apps before you go.

- Invest in a portable Wi-Fi hotspot if you need reliable internet on the move.

- Be mindful of data usage when using free Wi-Fi, especially for video streaming.

- Carry a power bank to keep your devices charged.

Additional Resources

- **WiFi Map:** This app helps you find Wi-Fi hotspots around the world, including Nice.

- **French mobile carrier websites:** Compare data plans and pricing before you buy a SIM card.

- **Nice Côte d'Azur Airport website:** Get the latest information on airport Wi-Fi services.

Useful Phrases

Greetings

- Bonjour (Hello)
- Salut (Hi)
- Enchanté(e) (Nice to meet you)
- Comment allez-vous ? (How are you?)

Asking for help

- Excusez-moi (Excuse me)
- S'il vous plaît (Please)
- Pourriez-vous...? (Could you...)
- Je ne comprends pas (I don't understand)
- Pouvez-vous répéter ? (Can you repeat that?)

Expressing gratitude

- Merci (Thank you)
- Merci beaucoup (Thank you very much)
- Je vous en prie (You're welcome)
- C'est gentil de votre part (Your kindness is appreciated.)

Making requests

- Puis-je avoir...? (May I have...)
- Pourriez-vous m'apporter...? (Could you bring me...)
- Je voudrais... (I would like...)
- Est-ce que c'est possible de...? (Is it possible to…)

Saying goodbye

- Au revoir (Goodbye)
- À bientôt (See you soon)
- Bonne journée (Have a good day)
- Bonne soirée (Have a good evening)

Additional phrases

- Oui (Yes)
- Non (No)
- Je suis désolé(e) (I'm sorry)
- Pardon (Excuse me)
- De rien (You're welcome)
- Félicitations (Congratulations)
- Bon appétit (Enjoy your meal)
- Santé (Cheers)

Emergency Contacts

General Emergencies

112: This is the European emergency number and can be used for any type of emergency, including fire, police, or medical assistance. It's free to call from any phone, even without a SIM card.

Specific Emergencies

- **17:** Police (gendarmerie) emergencies.
- **18:** Fire and medical emergencies. Firefighters in France are also equipped to handle medical emergencies.
- **196:** Maritime emergencies at sea.
- **114:** Emergency number for the deaf and hard of hearing.

Additional Resources

- **SOS Médecins:** Private on-call emergency care service. Doctors will come to your accommodation if you have a medical issue. Phone: 3624.
- **Nice Azur emergencies page:** Provides information on various emergencies and contact numbers.

Tips

- It's helpful to program these emergency numbers into your phone before you travel.

- If you don't speak French, try to stay calm and speak slowly and clearly when calling for help. Operators will usually be able to find someone who speaks English.

- Be aware of your surroundings and take precautions to avoid getting into dangerous situations.

ACCOMMODATION

Where to Stay

Le Negresco

- **Address: 37 Promenade des Anglais, 06000 Nice France**
- **Hotel Class: 5-star Hotel**

On the legendary French Riviera, Le Negresco is a timeless classic that is tucked away along the famous Promenade des Anglais and overlooks the magnificent Bay of Angels.

The essence of art and history painstakingly conserved by its owner, Jeanne Augier, from 1957 until 2019, is carried by this illustrious enterprise, one of the few independent luxury hotels in France. With more than 6,000 original pieces of art gracing the Hotel's hallways and suites, Madame Augier's legacy is carried on, providing each visitor with an immersive experience.

A voyage through the extraordinary eras from Louis XIII to the present is provided by Le Negresco's 102 rooms and 26 suites, each distinctively created and decorated with objects inspired by ages past. With nearly a century of history, the Hotel continues to be a symbol of quality, welcoming heads of state, performers, artists, and celebrities who have all added to the colorful tale that adorns it.

Beyond its opulent lodging, Le Negresco is a gourmet heaven with inventive and imaginative food handpicked by Best Craftsman Virginie Basselot. Visitors are in for a remarkable culinary experience, whether they choose to indulge in the Michelin-starred treats of Le Chantecler or to take in the ambiance of La Rotonde.

With real walnut woodwork going back to 1913, the Hotel's Bar welcomes guests to relax with a bite or beverage as the evening wears on, thumping to the sounds of jazz, pop, and soul. N La Plage, the recently opened private beach, beckons in the summer, providing a colorful setting for times spent in the sun overlooking the Bay of Angels.

Hotel De France, un hôtel AMMI

- **Location: 58 rue de France, 06000 Nice, France**
- **Hotel Class: 3-star Hotel**

Located only 150 meters from the glistening Mediterranean beaches and the well-known Promenade des Anglais, the charming Hotel de France *** is a hidden treasure. Whether it's a business trip or a private getaway, let me build a picture of the perfect hideaway for your next journey as your unofficial guide to the center of Nice's Carré d'Or.

Envision a location where each element has been thoughtfully chosen to guarantee your pleasure and comfort. In 2019, the Hotel had a complete makeover, emerging with a new look, a new elevator, and a welcoming patio. Imagine yourself relaxing on this patio, where the sun greets you with a delicious breakfast in the morning or the evening air invites you to have a leisurely drink in the evening.

Enter our cozy, compact rooms ***, each carefully planned and furnished with all the conveniences you may need to make the most of your stay. We've thought of everything, including a kettle, a Nespresso machine, and cozy bedding in addition to a mini-fridge. With separate air conditioning and soundproofing, enjoy the seclusion of your bathroom while staying connected with our 4G pocket Wi-Fi. A flat-screen TV puts entertainment at your fingertips, while an iron and hair dryer take care of the practicalities.

Hyatt Regency Nice Palais de la Mediterranee

- **Location: 13 Promenade des Anglais, Nice 06000, France**
- **Hotel Class: 5-star Hotel**

At the Hyatt Regency Nice Palais de la Mediterranee, discover an unrivaled world of elegance and comfort where each moment seems like a wonderful vacation. This sophisticated hideaway, tucked away in the center of Nice, is more than simply a hotel—it's a refuge for tired tourists looking to unwind and refresh.

A feeling of calm permeates this magnificent facility as soon as you walk in, guaranteeing that your stay will be nothing short of amazing. The rooms are tastefully decorated with contemporary facilities like minibars, air conditioning, and flat-screen TVs without sacrificing style for practicality. It's more than just lodging; it's a haven, a house away from home.

Beyond the rooms, the Hyatt Regency is dedicated to your well-being. Savor the ease of free Wi-Fi, which makes it simple to remain connected. A specialized concierge and room service are available to attend to all of your needs, making sure that your stay is smooth and worry-free.

Relax by the sparkling pool or in the cozy lounge after a day of visiting Nice's charming streets. This peaceful setting is ideal for telling stories about your travels. And don't worry, there are convenient parking facilities for those coming by vehicle.

With its prime location close to well-known sites like Place Masséna and Cathedrale Sainte-Reparate, the Hyatt Regency serves as your entryway into the heart of Nice. Take in the rich tapestry of the city and let every second be a learning experience.

At the Hyatt Regency, eating is transformed into an art form, but don't forget to check out the local restaurants for some amazing food. Acchiardo, Le Bistrot d'Antoine, and

La Petite Maison entice with the promise of delicious food only a short walk away.

Hôtel du Centre, un hôtel AMMI

- **Address: 2 rue de Suisse, 06000 Nice France**
- **Hotel Class: 2-star Hotel**

Conveniently located in the center of Nice, our quaint 2-star Hotel embraces guests with open arms and is a monument to comfort and convenience. Our sanctuary is a doorway to the alluring attractions of the French Riviera, perfectly located between the lively train station and the enthralling beach. Picture yourself waking up to the soft sound of the waves in the Mediterranean, adventure waiting just a short distance away.

After a 2018 renovation, our Hotel exudes a modern appeal while maintaining a welcoming, old-world feel. A stay that feels like a home away from home is ensured by the interiors, which are a beautiful combination of classic comfort and contemporary elegance. After a day of exploring the sun-kissed promenades or the historical treasures of Old Town, the rooms' exquisite design provides a peaceful haven.

The unique feature of our company is its excellent location, which makes getting to well-known places like Monaco, Cannes, Villefranche, and Antibes a breeze. Situated only a short distance away, the train station provides easy access to the French Riviera's jewels, enabling you to easily navigate the region's captivating landscape.

The Deck Hotel by HappyCulture

- **Address: 2 rue Maccarani, 06000 Nice France**
- **Hotel Class: 3-star Hotel**

At the magnificent The Deck Hotel by HappyCulture, a short distance from Nice's famous Promenade des Anglais, set off on a voyage of sophisticated luxury and seaside beauty. I'm excited to tell the captivating story of this stylish and sophisticated restaurant, having seen firsthand the captivating metamorphosis that occurs after six months of meticulous refurbishment.

The Deck Hotel invites you to enter a world of elegance and relaxation as soon as you walk through the door. The distinctive hallway, decorated in calming Mediterranean hues, creates the ideal atmosphere for an instantaneous escape into a world influenced by Greek mythology. This warm and bright sanctuary exists beyond the confines of daily existence.

The first-floor areas have a creative arrangement of light-colored walls that contrast with contemporary furniture, geometric textiles, and eye-catching suspensions. The furnishings, which skillfully combine modern style with the classic elegance of French hospitality, create a warm and fashionable atmosphere.

Reachable from any angle on the ground level, the terrace beckons you to a Greek-style retreat. It's a true stopover in Greece, offering moments of peace against the background of the turquoise sea. Wide doors open up to modest lounges decorated with cozy sofas and low tables.

Aparthotel AMMI Nice Massena

- **Address: 4 rue Massena, 06000 Nice France**
- **Hotel Class: 2-star Hotel**

Here at the charming Aparthotel AMMI Nice Massena, you can experience the best of Nice just outside your door. Imagine this: a peaceful retreat next to the famous Promenade des Anglais, the Place Massena, and the lush Albert 1st Gardens, all only three minutes' walk from the Mediterranean's blue embrace.

Our aparthotel is located in the center of Nice, like something straight out of a dream: a haven of tranquility among the lively bustle of the city. There are many ways to get about, and the proximity of trams, buses, and trains makes them the ideal starting point for exploring the city and its surroundings. Take in the local atmosphere; there are plenty of delicious eateries and quaint stores around.

Our apartments and studios are havens of luxury and comfort, not merely somewhere to stay. Every residence has a fully functional kitchenette, so feel free to fulfill your culinary fantasies. Enter your haven, replete with a well-thought-out bathroom, personal air conditioning to keep you comfortable, and double glazing to block off noise from the nearby metropolis.

Hotel de la Fontaine

- **Address: 49 rue de France, 06000 Nice, France**
- **Hotel Class: 3-star Hotel**

Situated in the vibrant center of Nice, only a short distance from the famous Promenade des Anglais and the turquoise waters of the Mediterranean, Hotel de La Fontaine serves as an entrance to a captivating realm just waiting to be discovered. Imagine this: the bustling pedestrian strip with its plethora of treasures, from quaint shops to busy cafés, is only a leisurely 100 meters away, beckoning you to immerse yourself in the beat of the city.

As someone who has personally experienced the attraction of this energetic city, I can vouch for the fact that Hotel de La Fontaine provides more than simply lodging. Each of the 29 rooms, which are works of art with unique patterns and hues, has been tastefully renovated to provide a cozy and fashionable retreat. Every element, like the anti-allergy flooring and the UPVC double-glazed windows that frame city views, was created with your enjoyment in mind.

Modern comforts like personal air conditioning, LCD TVs with satellite reception, and free Wi-Fi harmoniously coexist with classic elegance in these well-designed areas. Enter your comfortable, smoke-free haven and enjoy peace as the sun sets.

Imagine enjoying a delicious buffet breakfast on the terrace next to the fountain to start your day, with the sound of the running water lulling you into adventure. After exploring for the day—whether it's by going shopping in the ancient town or relaxing on the neighboring beaches in the sun—relax with a well-earned drink at the Bar.

Le Méridien Nice

- **Location: 1 Promenade des Anglais, 06046 Nice, France**
- **Hotel Class: 4-star Hotel**

Set off on a luxurious and elegant adventure to explore Le Méridien Nice, a masterpiece tucked away along the famous Promenade des Anglais. Imagine yourself lost in the classic elegance of the French Riviera, where leisure blends with refinement in the center of the Côte d'Azur.

Situated at No. 1 Promenade des Anglais, this contemporary Hotel is a shining example of comfort and flair. It is conveniently close to the charming Nice Old Town. I extend an invitation to you, as a witness to the charms of Le Méridien Nice, to bask in the alluring embrace of the Mediterranean Sea from any of the 318 opulent guest rooms, including 15 suites. Every area has been carefully designed to take you back to the glitzy 1960s while reflecting the diverse cultural heritage and urban allure of the area.

The breathtaking vistas that greet you as soon as you enter our family-friendly paradise will enthrall you. Imagine enjoying inventive drinks at Latitude Bar, where sophisticated foreign and local tastes coexist harmoniously. Head to the rooftop for La Terrasse, where fine cuisine meets breathtaking views of the Baie des Anges in an experience that's above and beyond ordinary.

Hotel West End

- **Address: 31 Promenade des Anglais, 06000 Nice France**
- **Hotel Class: 4-star Hotel**

Constructed in 1842 during the prestigious Belle Époque period, the West End Hotel is a brilliant jewel in the magnificent fabric of Nice's history. Say you could go back in time to a period when luxury ruled the globe and the French Riviera appealed to the nobility looking for a seaside vacation. This graceful Hotel, set along the legendary Promenade des Anglais, has emerged as a reminder of that bygone era.

You're not just walking into a hotel when you enter the West End—you're walking through time. The West End, which has its roots in the 19th century, is the epitome of tradition, savoir-faire, and modernity. The walls themselves appear to mutter stories of past parties when people laughed in front of the blue Mediterranean.

Well located, this charming home is just a five-minute walk from the ancient city's winding passages, an enthralling labyrinth that holds the mysteries of Nice's history. If you are itching for the comforts of modernity or dreaming of distant escapades, you will find that the airport and the Palais des Congrès meeting center are just a leisurely 10 minutes away.

Best Western Plus Hotel Brice Garden Nice

- **Location: 44 Marechal Joffre Street, Nice 06000, France.**
- **Hotel Class: 4-star Hotel**

Welcome to Nice, a charming city in the Mediterranean region, where the Best Western Plus Brice Garden is your refuge. Imagine a little hotel tucked away moments from the famous "Promenade des Anglais," the sun-kissed beaches, and the lively pedestrian lanes lined with unique stores and mouthwatering eateries.

The lively Place Massena, the ancient Vieux Nice (Old Town), and the busy Nice-Ville Railway Station are all easily accessible from this lovely haven. It's a clever cocoon that lets you easily get fully immersed in the spirit of the city.

Permit me to impart the spirit of the Best Western Plus Brice Garden as a witness to the attractiveness of this getaway. Your comfort is our first focus, with 59 roomy and welcoming suites, including contemporary conveniences like air conditioning, a fully stocked minibar, a personal safe, and free Wi-Fi. Picture yourself waking up on your balcony to the soft light of the Cote d'Azur sun, the ideal location for soaking up the distinct ambiance of the French Riviera.

NEIGHBORHOODS AND DISTRICTS

Old Town (Vieux Nice)

Take a trip back in time to the quaint Old Town of Nice, sometimes referred to as Vieux Nice, where the cobblestone streets whisper stories of bygone eras. Allow me to describe this charming neighborhood in graphic detail as a witness to the city's fascinating past.

Vieux Nice has a timeless beauty and is a tapestry of hues, a maze-like system of little streets decorated with colorful façades and hanging laundry. The aromas of locally prepared food and freshly baked pastries blend to create an auditory symphony that directs your investigation.

The bustling Cours Saleya, a vibrant market area where the aroma of fresh fruit, flowers, and spices fills the air, is the beating heart of Vieux Nice. Locals and tourists alike congregate here to peruse the outdoor market, choosing from a variety of fresh flowers or indulging in some of the area's best cuisine.

Go farther into the labyrinth of alleyways. You'll come across undiscovered treasures such as Place Rossetti, a charming area encircled by pastel-colored structures and overshadowed by the majesty of Cathédrale Sainte-Réparate. Get lost in the winding hallways, where every corner reveals a quaint café, a shop with handcrafted goods from the area, or a secret garden that takes you back in time.

Promenade des Anglais

A famous gem that adorns Nice's blue coastline, the Promenade des Anglais is a vast tapestry of beauty, history, and energetic energy. This palm-lined promenade, which flows gently down the Mediterranean, is the pulsating core of the city's attraction and is more than just a pretty promenade.

The Promenade des Anglais is a promenade where time appears to stand still. It is named after the English nobility who first visited the Riviera in the 18th century. Its broad breadth is lined on one side by magnificent Belle Époque architecture, opulent hotels, and quaint cafés, and on the other by the Mediterranean's azure seas, which gently lap against pebble beaches.

The promenade is a sensory extravaganza as well as a walkway. A distinct Niçois ambiance is created by the scent of freshly baked pastries mingling with the salty sea wind. Its embrace brings comfort to both locals and tourists, whether they are taking a leisurely walk, jogging along the shoreline, or just lounging in the warmth of the Mediterranean sun.

Important historically, Nice's Promenade des Anglais was a witness to the city's cultural resurgence in the 19th century and came to represent wealth and refinement. It still serves as a hub for culture and society today, presenting parades, festivals, and a close-up view of Nice's lively daily life.

Port of Nice

With its charming scenery and vibrant marine life, the Port of Nice, a busy nautical entryway to the French Riviera, entices tourists. This harbor, which is tucked away between the vivid metropolis and the blue seas of the Mediterranean, effortlessly combines historical relevance with contemporary beauty.

The sight of yachts and bobbing boats in the bay provides a mesmerizing scene as you go closer. The harbor is evidence of Nice's reputation as a playground for the wealthy and a sanctuary for marine enthusiasts, housing anything from modest private yachts to the boats of local fishermen.

The Port of Nice has historically been essential to the growth of the city, acting as a center for trade and observing the ebb and flow of many cultural influences. It still serves as a vibrant representation of Nice's multiculturalism today.

With palm palms and quaint cafés along it, the waterfront promenade is a great place for strolls and offers expansive views of the harbor and the glittering Mediterranean beyond. Charming seafood eateries around the quays entice onlookers with the prospect of delectable cuisine and fresh catch.

The Old Town, which is close to the harbor and has lively marketplaces and little lanes, makes it easy to get from the bustle of the sea to Nice's ancient center. Take boat tours from the Port of Nice to explore the stunning coastline, or just take in the vibrant environment that perfectly captures the essence of the French Riviera. The Port of Nice welcomes you to set off on a voyage where the beauty of the sea meets the charm of this coastal treasure, regardless of your interests in travel, culture, or the water.

Cimiez

Cimiez is a quiet, ancient area that is tucked away on the sun-kissed hillsides above Nice. It provides a fascinating diversion from the bustling activity of the city below. This upmarket neighborhood, which is well-liked by both residents and astute visitors, reveals a mosaic of ethnic diversity, lush surroundings, and an insight into Nice's glorious history.

With the archeological site of Cemenelum, an old Roman city from the first century AD, Cimiez is well known for its Roman past. Explore the well-preserved remains here, which include a theater and Roman baths, for a dramatic look into the city's past.

Beyond its archeological finds, Cimiez has tasteful Belle Époque residences surrounded by well-kept gardens and tree-shaded roads. The neighborhood has a classy vibe, which makes it a popular place to live for those looking for peace and expansive views of the Mediterranean.

Cimiez's cultural attractions, which include the famous Marc Chagall National Museum and the Matisse Museum, should provide comfort to art fans. These establishments are home to a sizable collection of pieces created by these accomplished artists, enabling guests to fully engage with the artistic fabric that characterizes the area.

Discover the harmony of the past and present as you stroll through Cimiez's lovely streets, which are bordered by blossoming flowers and shaded by old olive trees. Cimiez is a peaceful haven that invites you to experience the cultural richness and scenic vistas that characterize this upmarket getaway in Nice, whether you're looking to take in the architectural magnificence, learn about ancient history, or just relax and take in the artwork.

Mont Boron

With a breathtaking view of the Mediterranean Sea, Mont Boron is a natural gem perched above Nice's expansive terrain. This lush, green hill provides guests a chance to escape into the embrace of nature and enjoy unmatched views of the French Riviera.

A tapestry of pine and olive trees is revealed as one ascends Mont Boron, evoking a calm mood that seems worlds apart from the bustling cities below. The ascent is rewarded with breathtaking views that create a visual symphony between the lush green of the country and the vibrant blue of the sea, broken up by the red-tiled roofs of charming houses.

The famous Fort du Mont Alban, a medieval fortification from the sixteenth century, is one of Mont Boron's crown jewels. This well-preserved bastion provides an intriguing background to the picturesque splendor that surrounds Mont Boron and provides a window into the military history of the area.

Sunset lovers will find Mont Boron to be a wonderful spot as the sun sets, spreading its warm colors over the horizon. For those who are lucky enough to see it, the twinkling lights of Nice and the surrounding villages come to life, producing a picture-perfect scene that ingrains itself into their memories.

More than just a physical height, Mont Boron is a sanctuary for hikers, wildlife lovers, and anybody looking for a peaceful getaway with a dash of history. Its charm is found in the feeling of tranquility and timelessness that envelops tourists and beckons them to immerse themselves in the natural beauty that embodies the French Riviera, in addition to the stunning vistas.

SIGHTSEEING AND LANDMARKS
Castle Hill (Colline du Château)

Located in the center of Nice, with sweeping views of the blue Mediterranean and the charming cityscape, is the ancient Castle Hill, also known as the "Colline du Château." Not only has a view, this lofty sanctuary whispers stories of conquered, metamorphoses, and Nice's eternal soul, revealing the mysteries of bygone eras.

Despite the dismantling of the castle atop the peak in the 18th century, the remaining ruins serve as quiet reminders of the strategic importance this location has maintained throughout history. Castle Hill is a pleasant surprise for tourists today, providing a peaceful haven in the middle of the bustling metropolis as well as a trip through time.

There's a peaceful oasis at the top of the winding paths that are shrouded by abundant vegetation. Discovering secret corners and crevices that inspire reflection and awe is a pleasant exploration of the voyage. A stunning vista that perfectly encapsulates the spirit of the French Riviera awaits you when you reach the peak. Wide-ranging views of the bustling Old Town, the Promenade des Anglais, and the yachts dotted along the Mediterranean shore.

A well-known waterfall that plunges down the rocks at the summit of Castle Hill lends the ancient site a touch of natural splendor. Visitors are urged to stop and take in the place's ageless vitality through the cool mist and the calming sound of running water, which combine to create a tranquil mood.

Historical buffs may learn more about the medieval buildings that once adorned this impressive site by visiting the archeological site situated atop the hill. Much may be learned about the defenses that surrounded Nice from the ruins of old walls and foundations.

Museums and Art Galleries

Museums

Marc Chagall National Museum

- **Address: Av. Dr Ménard, 06000 Nice, France**

Visit the Marc Chagall National Museum in the enchanting hilltop suburb of Cimiez, Nice, to go on a visual voyage through the artist's creative universe. This artistic sanctuary is home to the largest collection of works by the French artist Chagall, who was born in Belarus, allowing guests to immerse themselves in the vibrant tapestry of his creative brilliance.

Admire the extraordinary collection of paintings, sculptures, stained glass, and tapestries, among other creative expressions, contained inside the museum's walls. A story that is timeless and ethereal is woven through every brushstroke, every minute detail of Chagall's sculptures, and the vivid colors of his stained glass windows.

The museum, which is perched high in Cimiez, offers a visual feast in addition to showcasing Chagall's talent. An additional element of charm to the whole experience is added by the hilltop location, which offers tourists breathtaking vistas of the city below and the glittering Mediterranean Sea.

Musée Matisse

- **Address: 164 Av. des Arènes de Cimiez, 06000 Nice, France**

Henri Matisse was a well-known French artist, and the Musée Matisse, located in the quiet area of Cimiez, is a fascinating example of his creative talent. This museum, a haven for fine art enthusiasts, provides a deep dive into the thoughts of one of the most significant artists of the 20th century.

The museum, which is solely devoted to honoring Matisse's legacy, is home to an enthralling collection that covers the artist's varied and remarkable career. Each work reveals a different aspect of Matisse's creative development, from vivid paintings that dance with color to the beautiful lines of sculptures, detailed drawings, and skillful prints.

Entering the Musée Matisse is like going inside the artist's temple. The meticulously chosen selection not only demonstrates the range of his creative abilities but also divulges the personal anecdotes and feelings that influenced his works. Witnessing the development of Matisse's style from his early pieces to the audacious experimentation that characterized his latter time is made possible by the museum, which offers a unique chance.

Musée d'Art Moderne Et d'Art Contemporain (MAMAC)

- **Address: Place Yves Klein, 06000 Nice, France.**

The Musée d'Art Moderne Et d'Art Contemporain (MAMAC), tucked away in the bustling center of Nice, is a symbol of the city's dedication to creative innovation. MAMAC is a sanctuary for lovers of modern and contemporary art, drawing guests in with a carefully chosen collection that captures the spirit of creative development. You are taken to a universe where imagination is unrestricted as soon as you enter.

Masterworks by some of the most significant painters of the 20th century, such as the well-known pieces by Picasso, Léger, and Dubuffet, are housed in MAMAC's meticulously selected galleries. These artists' brushstrokes come to life, creating a story that captures the vibrant spirit of modernism and the avant-garde.

MAMAC is ideally situated next to the famous Place Masséna and seamlessly integrates into Nice's diverse cultural landscape. The museum's proximity to this busy plaza adds even more attractiveness, beckoning art fans and curious bystanders to explore the always-changing terrain of modern innovation.

Art Galleries

Galerie des Ponchettes

- **Address: Quai des Etats-Unis, 06300 Nice, France**

The Galerie des Ponchettes is a shining example of modern art on the French Riviera, tucked away in the charming Port of Nice. The dynamic world of contemporary creativity is open for exploration by art fans and curious passersby at this little gallery.

Entering the Galerie des Ponchettes, you'll be engrossed in a vibrant exhibition of modern art. The walls are adorned with sculptures, paintings, and provocative installations, each adding to the kaleidoscope of creative expression.

With its window into the cutting edge of contemporary developments and trends, the gallery is a monument to the dynamic character of the art world.

The Galerie des Ponchettes is particularly engaging because of its dedication to showcasing emerging artists. The area creates an atmosphere where creativity is unrestricted by providing a stage for up-and-coming artists to convey their viewpoints. Viewers are given an intimate look at the cutting-edge and get to see the emergence of new creative voices that might have a big impact on the art industry in the future.

Galerie Masséna

- **Address: 65 Rue de France, 06000 Nice, France.**

The Galerie Masséna is a cultural gem in the center of Nice, tucked away behind the elegant walls of the Villa Masséna. The gallery, which offers visitors an immersive trip through time and creative expression, is housed in a stunning Belle Époque home that is a testimony to the architectural beauty of the period.

The Galerie Masséna is set against the magnificent background of the Villa Masséna, which is significant historically and architecturally. Entering through its doors, you are welcomed into a realm where ancient artifacts and modern art coexist together. Offering a rich tapestry of creative experiences, the gallery is a dynamic platform that showcases a broad selection of shows that engage and challenge.

The Galerie Masséna offers something for every creative taste, whether you are attracted to the bold brushstrokes of contemporary masterpieces or long for the nostalgic echoes of past times found in historical displays. Every display takes place within the villa's sacred corridors, fostering conversation between the past and the present.

Nicetoile Galeries

- **Location: 20 Rue de France, 06000 Nice, France.**

The lively tapestry of creative expression that the Nicetoile Galeries, tucked away in the busy center of Nice, captivates both residents and visitors with its alluring fusion of creativity. This art center, which provides a haven for local and international artists to weave their tales on canvas and in sculpture, is a tribute to the city's vibrant cultural scene.

The varied artwork on show at the Nicetoile Galeries brings the city of Nice to life, acting as a crossroads of cultures. Within this creative haven, the galleries serve as windows into the communal imagination. They are a mosaic of hues and shapes that convey stories of inventiveness, passion, and the global language of art.

This enthralling center crosses boundaries and creates a space where new abilities are recognized and supported. It is a haven for anyone looking for novel viewpoints, avant-garde expressions, and voices that push the frontier of creative conversation. Stepping into Nicetoile Galeries takes tourists on an exploratory adventure that goes beyond traditional art venues in terms of visual odyssey.

Promenade du Paillon

The Promenade du Paillon, a colorful paradise that winds through Nice, is tucked away in the center of the city and provides a welcome respite from the bustle of the city. This long promenade, which flows elegantly from the famous Place Masséna to the tranquil Promenade des Arts, is a symbol of the city's dedication to public parks and leisure time.

The Promenade du Paillon welcomes you with a symphony of colors, scents, and the soft patter of leaves from the verdant foliage that lines the walkway. A beautifully designed sanctuary, the promenade invites both residents and guests to enjoy the peace it offers with its well-balanced mix of plants, water features, and open areas.

Playful water jets that move in coordinated patterns invite kids to play and splash about, fostering a happy and energetic environment. Friends take a break on the many seats dotted around the promenade while families enjoy picnics on the immaculate grounds.

Sculptures and art installations provide the environment with an additional layer of cultural depth and create a sensory experience that goes beyond the typical. In addition, the linear park provides a lively setting for neighborhood gatherings, performances, and celebrations that infuse the city with a spirit of harmony and joy.

The Promenade du Paillon is a living mural that captures the spirit of Nice, not merely a green area. The promenade unifies the contemporary and ancient aspects of the city, surrounded by architectural wonders such as the Acropolis Convention Centre and the Museum of Contemporary and Contemporary Art (MAMAC).

Place Masséna

Place Masséna is a mesmerizing and distinctive plaza that seamlessly blends history, culture, and modernity. It is located in the center of the energetic city of Nice. This large square is the vibrant hub of the city, drawing both residents and tourists to enjoy its lively atmosphere with its eye-catching red-ochre buildings and checkerboard-patterned pavement.

Place Masséna is a tasteful fusion of modern and Belle Époque architecture, surrounded by chic shops, cafés, and palm palms. The sun dances on the orange and red façade of the buildings, creating a warm glow that reflects the essence of the French Riviera, and the plaza itself seems to be charged with a magnetic force.

Place Masséna is a hub for social events and meetings, and it holds a variety of celebrations all year long. The area comes to life with vibrant parades and lively musical performances that capture the joie de vivre of the Niçois. It's a location where residents and visitors come together to create a mosaic of laughter, languages, and special moments under the clear blue Mediterranean sky.

A touch of grandeur is added by the imposing Fontaine du Soleil, a gigantic statue in the middle of the plaza. With statues of Earth, Mars, Venus, and Mercury adorning it, this fountain serves as a charming meeting place or a resting place for people.

Place Masséna changes when day gives way to darkness. A captivating show of colorful lights fills the area, evoking a mystical mood. The atmosphere changes, and the area is transformed into a charming setting for strolls in the evening, friendly talks, and the odd street show.

ACTIVITIES IN NICE

Beaches and Waterfront

Beaches

- **Promenade des Anglais:** This iconic 7km stretch is Nice's most famous beach, offering stunning views of the Baie des Anges. It's perfect for sunbathing, people-watching, and strolling. Public sections mingle with private beach clubs, each offering sunbeds, umbrellas, and sometimes watersports.

- **Coco Beach:** A smaller, chic pebble beach with crystal-clear waters and a relaxed atmosphere. Rent a sunbed and sip cocktails at the beachside bar, or try your hand at paddleboarding.

- **Centenaire Beach:** Another public pebble beach with calmer waters, ideal for families with children. It boasts amenities like showers, changing rooms, and a playground.

- **Castel Beach:** Nestled at the foot of Castle Hill, this secluded cove offers a more intimate setting. Enjoy swimming in the turquoise waters or explore the charming Old Town nearby.

Waterfront

- **Port Lympia:** Nice's bustling harbor offers boat tours, yacht spotting, and fresh seafood restaurants. Take a scenic cruise along the coast or hop on a ferry to Cannes or Monaco.

- **Cours Saleya:** This lively flower market spills onto the waterfront every morning, a feast for the senses with vibrant blooms and the aroma of local produce.

- **Quai des Etats-Unis:** A picturesque promenade lined with palm trees and cafes, perfect for an afternoon stroll or a sunset drink with a view.

Beyond the beach

- **Promenade du Paillon:** A green oasis in the heart of the city, this landscaped park stretches all the way to the sea. Enjoy a picnic under the trees, rent a bike, or visit the MAMAC modern art museum.

- **Colline du Chateau:** Hike up to Castle Hill for breathtaking panoramic views of the city and the coastline. Explore the ancient castle ruins and stroll through the beautiful gardens.

Tips

- The best time to visit Nice for beach weather is from May to September.
- Public beaches are free, while private beach clubs charge for sunbeds and umbrellas.
- Nice has a well-developed public transportation system, making it easy to get around without a car.

Shopping Districts

For Luxury Retail

- **Le Carré d'Or (Golden Square):** This area around Rue Paradis and Avenue de Verdun glitters with luxury brands like Louis Vuitton, Chanel, Cartier, Armani, and Hermès. Prepare for luxury and high price tags.
- **Avenue Jean Médecin:** The main pedestrianized street in Nice boasts flagship stores of popular brands like Sephora, Mango, and Zara, alongside independent boutiques offering designer labels.

For Local Charm

- **Old Nice:** Wander through the maze of narrow streets in Nice's historic heart. Discover unique antiques, local crafts, and souvenir shops, as well as charming cafes and restaurants.

- **Place Garibaldi Antique Market:** Soak up the atmosphere of this lively square, where vendors display an eclectic mix of antiques, vintage clothing, and collectibles. Great for finding unique treasures.

For a Mix of Experiences

- **Nicetoile:** This large shopping mall combines major department stores (Galeries Lafayette) with international brands, local shops, and restaurants. Find something for everyone under one roof.

- **Marche St. Francois:** Immerse yourself in the daily life of Nice at this bustling fish market. Witness the vendors' hustle and bustle, and pick up some fresh seafood or local delicacies.

Bonus

- **Les Puces de Nice (Flea Market):** Hunt for bargains and hidden gems at this sprawling flea market, which is open on Sundays and Thursdays. You might find anything from furniture and antiques to vintage clothing and collectibles.

- **Marche Artisanal Nocturne (Summer Night Crafts Market):** During the summer months, discover handcrafted jewelry, artwork, and other creations at this charming evening market in Place Masséna.

Local Markets

Cours Saleya Flower Market

- **Address: Quai des États-Unis & Cours Saleya, 06300 Nice, France**
- **Open: Daily except Mondays, 7:00 am - 1:00 pm (peak season) or 6:00 pm (off-season)**

Discover the essence of Nice's Old Town at the Cours Saleya Flower Market, a dazzling sight of vivid colors and alluring scents. Every day, this famous market transforms the Promenade des Anglais into a sensory riot of colors and aromas that delight both residents and visitors. This old waterfront is transformed into a flowering paradise by the market, a vibrant event that takes Place every Monday.

Get ready to be mesmerized by the visual symphony of delicate violets, vivid geraniums, and the golden appeal of rich sunflowers as you walk among the market booths. The heavy perfume of roses in full bloom mingles with the sweet, delicate tones of lavender to create an enticing combination of scents that fill the air. The Cours Saleya Flower Market honors the color pallet of nature and is more than just a market area.

Liberation Market

- **Address: Place Charles de Gaulle, 06300 Nice, France**
- **Open: Tuesdays, Thursdays, and Saturdays, 7:00 am - 1:00 pm**

Get a taste of the lively local pace of life every Tuesday, Thursday, and Saturday morning at the Liberation Market, a busy, real food paradise that turns Place Charles de Gaulle into a sensory paradise. This is a vibrant display of Nice's culinary pulse, not simply a market.

The smell of fresh vegetables fills the air as you walk among the bustling booths, and you can hear the vibrant conversation of the Niçois. Take in the bright environment while browsing a variety of booths decked out in a rainbow of hues, with vivid fruits, crunchy veggies, shimmering fish, and handcrafted breads that entice with mouthwatering aromas.

Savor regional specialties like the rustic Socca, a chickpea pancake that captures the spirit of Niçois cuisine, or the savory pissaladière, an onion pie that entices the senses. These will allow you to fully immerse yourself in the region's rich cultural tapestry. Every mouthful takes you on a gourmet tour through the rich history of the French Riviera.

Marché Antique de Nice

- **Address: Quai de la Douane, 06300 Nice, France**
- **Open: Every Friday morning, 9:00 am - 5:00 pm**
- **Closed: Thursdays and Saturdays**

Take a trip back in time at the Marché Antique de Nice, a magical event that takes Place every Friday morning on the charming Quai de la Douane. This outdoor market invites residents and guests to immerse themselves in a historical treasure trove and an enthralling investigation of ancient times.

A rainbow of antiques and vintage treasures appears before your eyes as you browse the market's booths. Every piece, from gorgeous furniture and classic paintings to fine jewelry and sophisticated apparel, has a story from a bygone era. It's a sanctuary for those who are passionate about the past and have an eye for the future.

The vibrant atmosphere of discussion permeates the Marché Antique de Nice, elevating it beyond mere antiquities. Here, haggling is an art form—a dance between the buyer and the seller that amplifies the thrill of the transaction. This market is more than simply a location to shop; it's a theatrical production where every item you buy becomes a narrative and a palpable part of Nice's vibrant cultural fabric.

Place Garibaldi Market

- **Address: Place Garibaldi, 06300 Nice, France**
- **Open: Tuesdays, Thursdays, and Saturdays, 7:00 am - 1:00 pm**

Visit Place Garibaldi Market to immerse yourself in the vibrant tapestry of Nice's local life. This little area is teeming with bustle and ornamented with a rainbow of colorful buildings. Tuesdays, Thursdays, and Saturdays reveal a colorful metamorphosis as the square opens up into a thriving marketplace, inviting you to fully engage with the vivid energy of the city.

Wander among the several vendors selling a beautiful assortment of fresh fruit, colorful flowers, and trinkets made locally while the early sun warms the area. Savor the aroma of ripe fruits and aromatic flowers as you explore this multi-sensory experience. Savor the spirit of Nice with regional specialties like tapenade and Niçoise olives, which are a symphony of tastes that embodies the region's cuisine. In addition to being a marketplace, the market serves as a gathering place for culture, drawing both residents and tourists to enjoy the bounty of the Mediterranean way of life. Talk to the enthusiastic craftspeople who share their talents and create one-of-a-kind mementos that tell the tale of Nice. Every vendor offers an insight into the history of the city and an opportunity to bring a little bit of its colorful beauty home.

Cours Massena Flea Market

- **Address: Cours Masséna, 06300 Nice, France**
- **Open: Every Monday morning, 7:00 am - 1:00 pm**

Take a trip through time at the Cours Massena Flea Market, a magical scene that takes Place in the center of Nice every Monday morning. This vibrant market, which stretches over the famous Cours Massena and welcomes guests into a treasure trove of pre-owned treasures, is a paradise for both seasoned collectors and the curious.

A kaleidoscope of products surrounds you as you make your way through the market's colorful aisles, from eccentric furniture items that redefine nostalgia to antique apparel that whispers stories of bygone ages. As you peruse shelves brimming with home products that each have a unique tale to tell and tables covered with vintage trinkets, there's a thrilling sense of expectancy in the air.

The skill of closing a transaction is what distinguishes this flea market. Prepare your negotiating techniques as you interact with enthusiastic sellers who are happy to discuss the background of their products. The Cours Massena Flea Market is more than simply a place to buy; it's a vibrant marketplace where hidden jewels may be found among piled riches. It's a dance of bargaining.

Nightlife and Entertainment

1. **Bar hopping in the Old Town:** The narrow streets of the Old Town are lined with bars and pubs, making it a great place to wander and find a spot that suits your mood. There are dive bars, cocktail lounges, and everything in between. Start your crawl at Les Facteurs, a popular local spot with a great selection of beers on tap. Then, head to Wayne's Bar, a classic American-style pub with live music on weekends. If you're looking for something a little more upscale, try Mama Shelter Nice, a rooftop bar with stunning views of the city.

2. **Dance the night away at a nightclub:** Nice has a number of great nightclubs, many of which are located along the beachfront. If you're looking for something mainstream, check out Le Duplex or Le Crystal. For something a little more alternative, try La Suite or Black Pearl. And if you're really looking to let loose, head to Le Loft, a massive club that stays open until 6 am.

3. **Catch a show at the Nice Opera House:** The Nice Opera House is a beautiful Belle Époque theater

that hosts a variety of operas, ballets, and concerts throughout the year. It's a great option if you're looking for a more cultured night out.

4. **Try your luck at the Casino Nice:** The Casino Nice is a luxurious casino located in the heart of the city. It has a wide variety of gaming options, including slots, roulette, blackjack, and poker. There are also several restaurants and bars inside, so you can make a night of it.

5. **Enjoy a rooftop dinner with a view:** Nice has a number of great rooftop restaurants with stunning views of the city and the Mediterranean Sea. It's a great option for a special occasion or a romantic night out. Some of the best options include La Terrasse du Plaza, Molin, and Mama Shelter Nice.

CUISINE AND DINING

Traditional Niçois Cuisine

Traditional Niçois cuisine is a vibrant and flavorful blend of French and Italian influences. The use of fresh, seasonal ingredients, including olive oil, tomatoes, lemons, and herbs, characterizes it. Some. Some of the most popular Niçois dishes include:

1. **Salade Niçoise** is a classic salad that is made with tomatoes, cucumbers, onions, black olives, green beans, tuna, hard-boiled eggs, and anchovies. It is typically dressed with olive oil, lemon juice, and herbs.
2. **Soupe au pistou** is a hearty soup made with tomatoes, beans, and basil pesto. The pesto is made with basil, pine nuts, garlic, and olive oil.
3. **Pissaladière** is a savory flatbread that is topped with onions, anchovies, and olives. It is commonly cooked in a wood-fired oven.
4. **Socca** is a chickpea pancake that is cooked in a wood-fired oven. It is typically served with olive oil and herbs.
5. **Pan bagnat** is a stuffed sandwich that is made with tuna, anchovies, tomatoes, onions, hard-boiled eggs, and olives. It is typically served at room temperature.

Popular Restaurants

Chez Acchiardo

- **Address: 35 Rue Maccarani, 06000 Nice, France**
- **Open: Tuesday-Saturday: 12:00 pm - 2:00 pm & 7:00 pm - 9:30 pm, Closed Sunday & Monday**
- **Tel: +33 4 93 87 75 56**

Experience a gastronomic voyage at Chez Acchiardo, a Michelin-starred sanctuary created by the visionary chef Jean-Louis Acchiardo, right in the center of Nice. Chef Acchiardo, who is renowned for his culinary skills and dedication to providing mouthwatering sensations, has elevated eating to the status of an art form. Tucked away in the colorful mosaic of the city, this culinary treasure calls to both foodies and connoisseurs.

Traditional Provençal food is the main attraction of Chez Acchiardo, yet it's skillfully blended with a contemporary touch. Imagine a culinary symphony that dances across your senses, with every dish showcasing Chef Acchiardo's inventive brilliance. The atmosphere is as warm and welcoming as the food, which is varied and offers a wonderful blend of Nice's rich culinary history from the minute you walk in.

The Michelin star that befits Chez Acchiardo is more than just a badge of honor; it is evidence of the restaurant's everlasting devotion to the art of cooking and its steadfast commitment to perfection. Every dish is a work of art, painstakingly created to highlight the best ingredients and the creativity of the chef. Every mouthful is an adventure, whether you choose from the chef's tasting menu or choose one of the restaurant's hallmark dishes.

La Mere Germaine

- **Address: 22 Rue S. François de Paule, 06000 Nice, France**
- **Open: Daily: 12:00 PM - 2:30 PM & 7:00 PM - 10:00 PM**
- **Tel: +33 4 93 80 72 74**

At La Mere Germaine, a famous restaurant that has been a fixture in Nice's culinary scene since 1882, take a gastronomic trip through time. A real institution, this restaurant is a living example of the French Riviera's rich culinary legacy. Tucked away in the center of Nice, La

Mere Germaine entices a setting that combines the energy of modern cuisine with the allure of a bygone period.

The menu of La Mere Germaine honors the traditional Niçoise cuisine, which has been honed over many years in the kitchen. The scents of Socca, a crispy outside and soft, tasty inside of a delicious chickpea pancake, fill the air, luring you in to get a taste of Niçois heritage. Anchovies and olives adorning an onion pastry, called pissaladière, demonstrate the culinary skills passed down through the years.

Enjoy daube Niçoise, a beef stew cooked to perfection that fills the air with the aromatic scents of Provencal herbs, for a filling and cozy meal. At La Mere Germaine, every dish is a culinary tribute to the tastes of the area, meticulously maintained and delivered with a dash of classic elegance.

Le Bistro d'Antoine

- **Address: 2 Rue du Marché, 06000 Nice, France**
- **Open: Tuesday-Saturday: 12:00 pm - 2:30 pm & 7:00 pm - 10:00 pm, Closed Sunday & Monday**
- **Tel: +33 4 93 87 36 24**

Tucked away in the center of Nice, the lively Le Bistro d'Antoine is a gastronomic treasure that calls on residents and visitors alike to savor the classic tastes of French cooking. An ambiance that is in tune with the spirit of friendliness is created by the vibrant vibe that permeates the air.

A celebration of traditional French cuisine, Le Bistro d'Antoine's menu invites guests to experience the ageless charm of dishes that have graced tables for centuries. The flavor profile opens with the heady aromas of escargot, a specialty that perfectly embodies the spirit of classic French dining. A tempting fragrance of coq au vin, a rich stew of chicken stewed in red wine, fills the air as you browse the menu, promising a palate-pleasing symphony of flavors.

The steak frites offers itself as a gastronomic marvel to those looking for a classic French treat. A well-done steak combined with golden, crispy fries creates a harmonic harmony of flavors and textures that embodies the culinary genius of France.

Papilla

- **Address: 23 Rue Bonaparte, 06000 Nice, France**
- **Open: Tuesday-Saturday: 12:00 pm - 2:30 pm & 7:30 pm - 10:30 pm, Closed Sunday & Monday**
- **Tel: +33 4 93 80 27 51**

Visit Papilla, a modern sanctuary where the craftsmanship of fresh Mediterranean food is revealed, and go on a gastronomic adventure. Perched at the nexus of innovation and tradition, Papilla entices discriminating palates with its dedication to using local, fresh ingredients that blend well with each dish.

Enter a setting where culinary artistry and modernism coexist harmoniously. The chefs at Papilla create a dynamic menu that is a culinary canvas that transforms with the seasons to provide a constantly changing symphony of tastes. Expect a kaleidoscope of delicious selections while dining, including unique dishes that capture the spirit of the area.

Savor the exquisite fusion of tastes with pasta covered with seafood riches, a celebration of the aquatic treasures found across the Mediterranean. Enjoy the essence of elegance and simplicity as the flawlessly prepared grilled fish takes center stage, bringing out the natural flavor of every ingredient. The strong and earthy tastes of locally sourced produce are revealed with every mouthful, elevating the art of roasting vegetables to new heights.

Tippsy

- **Address: 6 Rue Masséna, 06000 Nice, France**
- **Open: Daily: 11:00 AM - 2:00 AM**
- **Tel: +33 4 93 80 07 93**

This beloved local treasure of a restaurant and bar has established a reputation as a destination for those looking for a unique fusion of creative drinks and mouthwatering tapas. The menu is a symphony of flavors that features a wide variety of small appetizers to suit all tastes.

Savor the savory and rich flavors of artisanal cheeses and carefully chosen charcuterie, masterfully combined to tempt your palate. Savor the perfectly crisp crostini, with each bite revealing a masterful work of culinary technique. The patatas bravas, a gastronomic marvel unto themselves, provide the ideal ratio of comfort and spice.

Every meal at Tippsy is an ode to culinary creativity, showcasing a dedication to finding the best ingredients and enhancing the eating experience. With each drink, the inventive cocktail menu invites customers to experience a new sense that goes well with the food.

Cafés and Bakeries

Emilie and the Cool Kids

- **Address: 11 Rue du Marché, 06300 Nice, France**
- **Open hours: Tuesday-Saturday 8:30 am - 6:30 pm, Sunday 10:00 am - 4:00 pm, closed Monday.**

Situated close to the busy Cours Saleya in the center of Nice, Emilie and the Cool Kids is a hip retreat that welcomes visitors and residents alike with its colorful embrace. For those looking for a great culinary experience, this little location is a must-visit, as it easily combines culinary brilliance with a trendy atmosphere.

With their mouthwatering selection of cakes, cookies, and coffee, Emilie and the Cool Kids have carved out a place for themselves. Each creation is the ideal fusion of taste and creativity. The inviting smell of freshly baked goods fills the air as soon as you walk through the door, preparing you for a delicious culinary adventure.

Warmth and trendiness blend to create a cozy environment inside. The young people behind the counter have a wonderful enthusiasm and greet customers with sincere grins and a love for what they do. The rooms create a trendy but pleasant atmosphere with their varied décor and vivid colors.

B-BAKER - Les Petits Pains de Méditerranée

Several locations in Nice; here are two popular ones:

1. **The address is 14 Rue Saint-François de Paule, 06300 Nice, France.**

2. **3 Rue Masséna, 06000 Nice, France**

- **Open hours: Monday- Saturday, 7:00 am - 7:30 pm; Sunday, 8:00 am - 6:30 pm. The duration of operation might experience slight variations based on the specific location.**

B-BAKER: Les Petits Pains de Méditerranée is a bakery chain that calls with the seductive scent of freshly baked delicacies. Take a gourmet adventure through the heart of Nice with them. Every Nice site offers a delicious blend of history and innovation, a veritable treasure trove of Mediterranean delicacies.

For those looking for a fast treat or a leisurely meal, B-BAKER is a sanctuary. Imagine yourself entering one of their quaint locations, where the aroma of freshly baked bread, golden pastries, and mouthwatering treats fills the air. You can sense the bakery's commitment to quality and freshness as soon as you walk in.

B-BAKER provides everything you could want, including warm, crispy baguettes, buttery croissants, and flavorful sandwiches. There is plenty on the menu to suit every taste, ranging from robust salads to traditional French pastries. Every Nice location has a distinct charm of its own, luring customers to enjoy their Mediterranean-inspired cuisine in a laid-back setting.

Patisserie Franck & Rosi

- **Address: 2 Rue Catherine Segurane, 06300 Nice, France**
- **Open hours: Tuesday-Saturday 7:00 am - 7:00 pm, Sunday 8:00 am - 6:00 pm, closed Monday.**

Embracing the rich tapestry of the city's culinary tradition, Patisserie Franck & Rosi is a beloved institution nestled in the heart of Nice. With a history that goes back decades, this classic bakery entices customers with the delicious smell of freshly made treats, an alluring call to indulge in the best bread, chocolates, and pastries that Nice has to offer.

Enter a world where sweets and art collide, where every item is a work of love and accuracy. The delicate layers of mille-feuille whisper stories of culinary skill, while the velvety richness of chocolates takes you to a land of pure enjoyment. Patisserie Franck & Rosi is a symphony of tastes.

This is more than just a bakery; it's a window into the heart of Nice, where residents and tourists alike come to sample the pinnacle of French pastry artistry. Every creation, from the rich eclairs to the painstakingly crafted chocolates, is proof of Franck & Rosi's commitment to their art.

Maison Auer

- **Address: 7 Rue Saint-François de Paule, 06300 Nice, France**
- **Open hours: Monday-Saturday 9:30 am - 7:00 pm, Sunday 10:00 am - 6:00 pm.**

Enter the enchanted realm of Maison Auer, a renowned restaurant that has been gracing Nice's streets since 1875. It's more than just a candy store; it's a living reminder of the delicious history of the city. Upon entering Maison Auer, the rich scent of candied fruits and the seductive appeal of rich chocolate instantly take you back in time.

Maison Auer is an expert in creating beautiful chocolates, candies, and fruits. They have perfected the art of striking the right mix between tradition and modernity. Their products are distinctly rooted in the local culture and embody the spirit of the sun-kissed Mediterranean. Key ingredients in their products include orange and lemon, which dance on the tongue like a symphony of tastes.

Beyond only confections, Maison Auer's workmanship pays respect to Nice's rich culinary history. Every treat has a backstory that is crafted using the best ingredients and time-tested methods. Not content to just sate one's sweet taste, Maison Auer's legacy is a celebration of the art of indulgence and a monument to the long-lasting love affair that exists between Nice and her delicious treasures.

Le Panier d'Emilie

- **Address: 4 Rue Saint-François de Paule, 06300 Nice, France**
- **Open hours: Tuesday-Saturday 8:00 am - 7:00 pm, Sunday 9:00 am - 6:00 pm, closed Monday.**

Le Panier d'Emilie, tucked away in the center of Nice, calls with the tantalizing smell of freshly baked goods and the prospect of a gourmet getaway. A hidden treasure among

Niçois pleasures, this little café enchants guests with its handcrafted charm and mouthwatering fare.

You'll enter Le Panier d'Emilie and be engulfed in a world of freshly created treats. The aroma of freshly baked goods, cakes, and tarts fills the air; each is made with care and attention to detail. The variety of sweets, which includes flaky pastries and velvety chocolate cakes, demonstrates the commitment to excellence that characterizes this company.

The menu is a symphony of tastes, offering a variety of savory indulgences such as sandwiches and salads in addition to mouthwatering desserts. Sophisticated palates will find paradise at Le Panier d'Emilie, whether they're in the mood for a simple meal or a luxurious dessert.

For those who love the concept of eating outside, the café has a little terrace that is a peaceful haven under the soft Mediterranean sun. Here, guests may enjoy their culinary treasures outside among the rustic appeal of wrought-iron chairs and potted flowers, which adds even more magic to the dining experience.

Cafe Carlina

- **Location: 14 Rue Saint-François de Paule, 06300 Nice, France**
- **Open hours: Monday- Saturday, 8:00 am - 8:00 pm; Sunday, 9:00 am - 7:00 pm.**

Tucked away in the center of the fascinating Old Town, Cafe Carlina entices with the promise of delicious culinary adventures. This little business has proven to be a treasured find and a popular choice for both residents and tourists looking for a gastronomic haven in the center of Nice.

A refuge for lovers of coffee, lunch aficionados, and breakfast, Cafe Carlina offers a warm ambiance that combines the freshness of contemporary food with the historic grandeur of the Old Town. The perfume of freshly made coffee and the delicious smell of Italian-inspired delights welcome you warmly as soon as you enter our gastronomic getaway.

With a wide variety of dishes inspired by Italy's rich culinary traditions, the menu at Cafe Carlina is a symphony of tastes. Every dish, from soul-satisfying pasta and colorful salads to delicious pizzas with flawlessly crispy crusts, is made with care and attention to detail. The chefs at Cafe Carlina take great pleasure in creating a cuisine that appeals to a wide range of palates, making every visit an adventure through a palate of mouthwatering experiences.

Food Festivals

1. **Refugee Food Festival:** This unique festival celebrates the culinary traditions of refugees and asylum seekers living in Nice. It features cooking demonstrations, workshops, and meals prepared by refugees from all over the world.

2. **Food tours:** There are several food tours available in Nice that take you to some of the city's best restaurants and markets. These tours are a great way to sample the local cuisine and learn about Niçoise food culture. Some popular food tours include "The Flavors of Nice Food Tour" and "The Flavors of Cannes Food Tour."

3. **Christmas markets:** While not strictly food festivals, Nice's Christmas markets do offer a variety of food and drink options. You can find everything from traditional French pastries and sausages to mulled wine and hot chocolate. The Christmas markets are open from late November to late December.

4. **Nice Carnival:** This world-famous carnival takes Place in February and features food stalls from all

over the world. It's a great opportunity to try some unique and delicious dishes.

5. **Fête du Citron (Lemon Festival):** This festival takes Place in Menton, just a short train ride from Nice, in February and March. It celebrates all things lemons with giant lemon sculptures, parades, and, of course, plenty of lemon-flavored food and drink.

6. **Gourmet Odyssey:** This festival takes Place in Nice in May and June and features cooking demonstrations, tastings, and workshops from some of the world's best chefs.

THING TO DO

Hiking Trails

For beginners

- **Coastal Path:** Nice - Villefranche-sur-Mer: This easy 4.6-kilometer trail offers stunning views of the Mediterranean Sea as you walk from Nice to the charming village of Villefranche-sur-Mer. The path is well-maintained and mostly flat, making it perfect for a stroll.

- **Promenade des Anglais:** This iconic 7-kilometer beachfront promenade is a great place for people to watch and enjoy the scenery. You can walk, bike, or rollerblade along the path, and there are plenty of cafes and restaurants to stop at along the way.

- **Colline du Château (Castle Hill):** This easy 2.2-kilometer hike takes you to the top of Castle Hill, where you'll be rewarded with panoramic views of Nice and the French Riviera. The climb is a bit steep in some sections, but there are plenty of places to rest along the way.

For intermediate hikers

- **Mont Boron - Mont Alban:** This moderate 6.5-kilometer hike takes you through the lush forests of Mont Boron and Mont Alban. The trail is well-marked and offers some challenging climbs, but the views from the top are worth it.
- **Vinaigrier Mountain:** This moderate 5.5-kilometer hike takes you to the top of Vinaigrier Mountain, where you'll find a 360-degree view of the surrounding area. The trail is a bit rocky in some sections, so be sure to wear good shoes.
- **Nice-Cannes:** This moderate 14-kilometer hike takes you from Nice to Cannes along the coastal path. The trail is well-marked and offers some challenging climbs, but the views of the Mediterranean Sea are amazing.

For experienced hikers

- **Mercantour National Park:** This national park is located in the mountains behind Nice and offers some of the best hiking in the region. There are trails for all levels of experience, from gentle walks to challenging climbs.

- **Chemin du Fenestre:** This difficult 28-kilometer trail is one of the most challenging hikes in the area. It takes you through the mountains of the Mercantour National Park and offers stunning views of the surrounding countryside.
- **Sentier des Douaniers:** This moderate 12-kilometer trail follows the old customs path along the coast between Nice and Menton. The trail offers some challenging climbs and beautiful views of the Mediterranean Sea.

No matter what your level of experience, there's a hiking trail in Nice that's perfect for you. Prepare your footwear and embark on the journey!

Here are some additional tips for hiking in Nice:

- Be sure to wear proper footwear and clothing, as the weather can change quickly in the mountains.
- Bring plenty of water and snacks, especially if you're going on a long hike.
- Let someone know where you're going and when you expect to be back.
- Stay vigilant of your environment and be cautious of wildlife in the vicinity.

- Respect the environment and leave no trace.

Water Sports

Nice, the crown jewel of the French Riviera, boasts a stunning coastline and calm Mediterranean waters, making it a paradise for water sports enthusiasts. Whether you're a seasoned adrenaline seeker or a curious beginner, there's something for everyone in Nice's aquatic playground.

Here's a glimpse into the exciting world of water sports in Nice:

For the thrill-seekers

- **Jet skiing:** Feel the wind whip through your hair as you carve across the waves on a powerful jet ski. Several operators along the Promenade des Anglais offer rentals and tours, with some even reaching the glamorous shores of Monaco.

- **Parasailing:** Soar high above the turquoise waters, enjoying breathtaking panoramic views of the city and the coastline. Parasailing is a great way to experience the beauty of Nice from a unique perspective.

- **Flyboarding:** Take your adrenaline levels to a whole new level with flyboarding. This exhilarating sport uses water pressure to propel you into the air, allowing you to perform flips and tricks like a superhero.
- **Scuba diving:** Explore the vibrant underwater world of the Mediterranean Sea. Nice offers numerous dive sites, from shipwrecks and coral reefs to hidden grottoes teeming with marine life.

For the relaxed souls

- **Stand-up paddleboarding (SUP):** Enjoy a leisurely paddle along the coast, soaking up the sunshine and the scenery. SUP is a great way to get some exercise while enjoying the tranquility of the water.
- **Kayaking:** Glide through the calm waters of Baie des Anges or explore the rocky coves around Cap de Nice. Kayaking is a fantastic way to discover hidden gems and enjoy the peacefulness of the sea.
- **Snorkeling:** Immerse yourself in the underwater world, marveling at colorful fish and vibrant coral reefs. Snorkeling tours are available for all levels,

making it a perfect activity for families and solo travelers alike.

Bonus

- **Boat tours:** Take a scenic boat tour along the coast, admiring the charming towns and picturesque landscapes of the French Riviera. Certain tour packages may even incorporate opportunities for swimming and snorkeling.

No matter what your level of experience or preferred pace, Nice has the perfect water sport for you. So, grab your swimsuit, sunscreen, and adventurous spirit, and get ready to make a splash in the turquoise waters of the French Riviera!

Remember, the best time for water sports in Nice is during the summer months, from May to September when the weather is warm and sunny. However, some activities like kayaking and stand-up paddleboarding are available year-round, depending on the weather conditions.

Cycling Routes

For beginners

- **The Promenade des Anglais:** This flat, 7km coastal path is perfect for a leisurely ride with stunning views of the Mediterranean Sea.

- **The Baie des Anges:** This sheltered bay is another great option for a relaxed ride, with plenty of cafes and restaurants to stop at along the way.

- **Le Bar-sur-Loup:** This charming village is a short 18km ride from Nice, and the surrounding countryside is perfect for a gentle climb.

For intermediate cyclists

- **Col de Vence:** This 128km loop with 2710m of climbing is a challenging but rewarding ride, with stunning views of the French Riviera from the top.

- **Col de la Madone:** This 101km loop with 2570m of climbing is another classic Nice climb, with a famous section that featured in the Tour de France.

- **Cannes and the Corniche de l'Esterel:** This 75km route takes in some of the most beautiful scenery on the Côte d'Azur, with dramatic cliffs and secluded coves.

For experienced cyclists

- **Col de la Bonette:** This 237km route with 7978m of climbing is the highest paved road in Europe and a real challenge for even the fittest cyclists.
- **Le Tour du Mont Blanc:** This epic 733km route circumnavigates Mont Blanc, the highest mountain in Western Europe, and is a must-do for any serious cyclist.
- **Nice to Monaco:** This short, 27km route is a great way to experience the glamour of Monaco, with stunning views of the city and the casino from the top of the climb.

FESTIVALS AND EVENTS

Nice Carnival

One of the most famous and vibrant festivities in the world is the Nice Carnival, a stunning display of color, inventiveness, and unbridled joy. Taking Place every year in Nice, which is tucked away on the sunny beaches of the

French Riviera, this festival turns the city into a carnival paradise that captivates both residents and tourists.

The Nice Carnival, which dates back to the thirteenth century, has developed into a lavish spectacle that is inspired by many cultures, historical events, and modern topics. Every year in February, just before Lent begins, the carnival explodes into life with a riot of color that dances over the blue sky.

The big parade, a captivating procession of intricate floats decked out in colorful flowers, feathers, and fanciful figures, is the centerpiece of the carnival. Massive papier-mâché figurines come to life, portraying a wide variety of subjects, from fantastical worlds to historical occurrences. The streets are alive with onlookers' shouts and laughing, and the air is filled with the contagious rhythms of music.

An iconic and cherished Nice Carnival custom is the "flower battles." Elegantly dressed participants, referred to as "Niçois," exchange flowers in a lighthearted manner at these vibrant festivities, producing a fragrant and bright sight. Combining the vibrant spirit of competition with the aesthetic attraction of flowers, the Battle of Flowers is a sensory extravaganza.

The carnival includes an array of street entertainment, exciting parties, and cultural activities in addition to parades and flower wars. Every area of Nice is filled with the colorful energy of the celebrations, which fosters a happy and festive environment.

With spectacular parades held at night, the celebrations continue as the sun sets over the Mediterranean, casting a mystical light over the city. Nice's dedication to maintaining customs, encouraging innovation, and extending an invitation to everyone to experience the pure joy of living on the French Riviera is shown by the annual Nice Carnival. Every year, Nice Carnival is an extraordinary event that invites everyone to experience the enduring charm of this captivating celebration.

Jazz à Juan Festival

The Jazz à Juan Festival, which takes Place every year on the French Riviera's sun-kissed coves, is a tribute to the perfect union of music and stunning scenery. From its start in 1960, this legendary jazz festival has brought music lovers and jazz connoisseurs from all over the globe to the little village of Juan-les-Pins, turning it into a worldwide platform.

The event takes place on the stunning Pinède Gould stage, which the blue Mediterranean Sea surrounds. This setting creates an unmatched atmosphere that is filled with the lyrical melodies of both up-and-coming jazz artists and jazz stalwarts. A legacy of musical invention is woven throughout the festival's history, including performances by legends like Ray Charles, Ella Fitzgerald, and Miles Davis.

Known as the "oldest jazz festival on the French Riviera," the Jazz à Juan Festival has established a reputation for outstanding performances and a lively environment. It's a celebration that embraces a wide range of jazz genres, from bebop to fusion, traditional to modern, and beyond time and genre borders.

Every July, jazz music fills the lively streets of Juan-les-Pins as eager audiences assemble to experience the electrifying power of live music. The event extends beyond the main stage to secluded taverns, jazz clubs, and beachside locations, giving visitors an immersive opportunity to discover the wide range of aspects of this musical style.

Jazz à Juan is unique because of its dedication to developing up-and-coming talent and giving the next wave of jazz virtuosos a stage on which to perform alongside titans of the field. The festival has an impact that goes beyond the music performed on stage; it promotes a lively cross-cultural interchange that enhances the French Riviera's creative milieu.

Jazz à Juan Festival is an annual pilgrimage for anyone looking to be transported by the timeless charm of Jazz on the sands of this lovely coastal town. As the sun sets over the Mediterranean, putting a warm light over the celebrations, the festival never fails to capture hearts and create lasting memories.

Bastille Day Celebrations

Celebrated on July 14th, Bastille Day is a magnificent example of France's spirit of independence, togetherness, and brotherhood. Honoring the storming of the Bastille prison in 1789, a momentous event in the history of the French Revolution, the day is celebrated with great fanfare throughout the country. In Nice, where Bastille Day is a spectacular spectacle that enthralls both residents and tourists, there is no greater place to experience the joy and excitement than this city.

The famous Promenade des Anglais, an appropriate venue for the activities' grandeur, is the center of the Nice festival. The promenade turns into a kaleidoscope of colors as the sun sets over the Mediterranean, and a spectacular fireworks show lights up the night sky. Along the shoreline, families, friends, and visitors congregate, fostering a joyful environment full of shared delight and laughter.

There's more to the celebration than just flashing fireworks. Parades, concerts, and cultural activities fill the city earlier in the day. Marching bands fill the air with upbeat music, and colorful floats, dancers, and entertainers flood the streets, all adding to the mosaic of French pride and legacy.

Bastille Day in Nice is a sensory extravaganza that culminates in a breathtaking fireworks show that reflects off the blue seas of the Mediterranean. The French flag's colors—red, white, and blue—are painted on the night sky with coordinated light blasts. People from all walks of life look up in unison, filled with amazement and happiness.

Bastille Day is an unmatched spectacle that not only honors a historic milestone but also highlights the continuing spirit of liberty and brotherhood that characterizes the essence of France, making it an unmatched experience for visitors looking for an amazing time in Nice. Enjoying the splendor of the French national holiday on the sunny beaches of the Côte d'Azur is an invitation that transcends time.

LOCAL ETIQUETTE AND CUSTOMS

Tipping Guide

Tipping customs in Nice are different from countries like the US, where it's expected. In France, including Nice, tipping is not mandatory and is considered a gesture of appreciation for good service. Here is a guide to assist you in navigating:

Restaurants

- Locals typically don't tip, but tourists often do out of habit.
- If you decide to tip, a small round-up to the nearest euro is customary, usually €1-2.
- For exceptional service, 5-10% of the bill is acceptable.
- Service charge (service compris) is sometimes included in the bill; check for "SC" or "service compris" before tipping.

Bars and Cafes

- Similar to restaurants, tipping is not expected but appreciated.

- For basic service, rounding up to the nearest euro is sufficient.
- For friendly and attentive service, consider €1-2.

Taxi

- Tipping is not common for taxis, but rounding up the fare is acceptable.

General Tips

- Always pay with cash for tips or ask if a credit card can be used for gratuity.
- Never feel obligated to tip; it's purely optional.
- Don't tip with coins; it's considered disrespectful.
- If unsure, observe how locals handle tipping to get a better feel.

Bonus

- Instead of tipping, consider expressing your thanks verbally with a sincere "merci beaucoup" (thank you very much). This is often appreciated by service staff.

Remember, tipping in Nice is more about showing appreciation than obligation. Relax, enjoy your time, and tip as you feel comfortable.

Cultural Do's and Don'ts

DO's

1. **Greet with a smile and bonjour:** Always greet locals with a friendly "bonjour" (hello) and a smile. It shows respect and makes a good first impression.

2. **Learn a few basic French phrases:** While English is spoken in some tourist areas, learning a few basic phrases like "merci" (thank you) and "s'il vous plait" (please) goes a long way.

3. **Embrace the pace of life:** A nice life revolves around leisure and enjoying the good things. Sit back, relax, and savor your meals, coffee, and conversations.

4. **Respect table manners:** French dining etiquette is important. Keep your elbows off the table, use the proper cutlery, and avoid rushing through your meal.

5. **Dress appropriately:** While Nice is casual, avoid overly revealing clothing, especially in churches or historical sites. Opt for smart casual attire for dining and nightlife.

6. **Explore beyond the beach:** Nice offers more than just beaches. Immerse yourself in the historic Old Town (Vieux Nice), visit museums like the Matisse Museum, or climb Castle Hill for stunning views.

7. **Sample the local cuisine:** Nice is a gourmand's paradise. Try Niçoise specialties like Socca (chickpea pancake), fresh seafood, and delectable pastries.

8. **Support local businesses:** Patronize local shops, markets, and cafes instead of large chain stores. It contributes to the local economy and adds to the authentic experience.

9. **Practice patience:** Things might move at a slower pace in Nice, especially during peak season. Embrace the laid-back attitude and avoid getting flustered.

DON'Ts

1. **Speak loudly or be boisterous:** The French value discretion and quiet enjoyment. Avoid speaking too loudly in public places or restaurants.

2. **Push personal boundaries:** Avoid asking personal questions about salary, family, or relationships unless you have a close relationship with someone.

3. **Litter or be disrespectful:** Keep Nice and clean and respect the environment. Don't litter or vandalize public property.

4. **Wear beachwear everywhere:** While bikinis and swimsuits are acceptable at the beach, they're not appropriate for sightseeing or dining.

5. **Be impatient with queues:** Lines can be long in tourist areas. Remain patient and avoid cutting in line.

6. **Expect fast service:** Restaurants and cafes prioritize the dining experience over speed. Enjoy the conversation and atmosphere, and don't expect a quick meal.

7. **Ignore dress codes:** Some restaurants might have dress codes, especially for dinner. Check beforehand or dress on the smarter side to avoid embarrassment.

8. **Forget to tip:** While tipping is not mandatory, leaving a small amount (around 5-10%) for good service is appreciated.

DAY TRIPS AND EXCURSIONS

Monaco

Take a day excursion from Nice to Monaco to see the riches of this little principality and the splendors of the French Riviera. You start your journey by leaving the bustling streets of Nice behind and traveling down the narrow coastal roads that hug the blue Mediterranean. With its expansive vistas of the glistening sea and striking cliffs, the picturesque drive alone is a sight to see.

When you arrive in Monaco, the city-state tucked away in the Maritime Alps, you'll be enthralled with its opulent atmosphere and stunning architecture. Begin your journey in the renowned Monte Carlo Casino, an icon of luxury that has adorned many motion pictures and stories of glamorous high-stakes gambling. This famous monument is made even more appealing by the surrounding gardens and Belle Époque architecture.

Make your way to the Prince's Palace, which is situated atop Monaco's Rock, as you stroll around the city. Admire the imposing stronghold, and if you're lucky, you may see the event known as the Changing of the Guard, which is a relic of centuries of royal past.

The Monaco Oceanographic Museum has a hint of maritime magic. This institution, set into the cliffs, has informative exhibitions and captivating aquariums that highlight marine life. Larvotto Beach, which is close by, invites you to enjoy a tranquil getaway and soak up the Mediterranean sun.

A visit to the famous Jardin Exotique is a must-do while visiting Monaco. This lush garden has a wide variety of succulents and cacti from all over the globe and is set on a cliffside with stunning views of the city.

Explore the quaint alleyways of La Condamine, which is well-known for its lively markets and inviting cafés, as the day comes to an end. Enjoy regional specialties and maybe get a look at the superyachts berthed in the port here.

Retracing your steps to Nice as the sun sets is a contemplative experience that fills you with memories of a day spent in a principality that skillfully combines luxury, history, and scenic beauty. It's a day excursion that stays in your heart long after the lights of Monaco disappear from your rearview mirror.

Cannes

Take a captivating tour that reveals the disparate sides of the French Riviera in a single day as you go from the energetic streets of Nice to the glitzy charm of Cannes. The coastline is very beautiful, and a picturesque drive of around thirty kilometers displays it as the blue Mediterranean extends beside the road.

When one first arrives in Cannes, the refinement that characterizes this famous city captivates them. Cannes, well-known for its yearly film festival, has a glamorous and exclusive vibe. Start your tour by meandering around the well-known Boulevard de la Croisette, which is surrounded by palm trees, posh stores, and promenades that weave an exquisite tapestry of shops. The Mediterranean sun is warm and inviting on the sandy beaches, which provide a striking contrast to Nice's pebbly shoreline.

Explore Cannes's historic center by heading into the Old Town or Le Suquet. Charming squares are crossed by cobblestone streets that take you to the hilltop medieval stronghold. Offering a brief respite in the middle of the busy Riviera, the vantage point offers expansive views over the city and the Lerins Islands.

A trip to the Film Festival Palace is a must-do while in Cannes. The legendary red carpet and the handprints of well-known movie stars immortalize the splendor and glamor of this famous event. Explore the world of film at the nearby Film Festival Museum, where displays honor the cinematic medium.

Savor the gastronomic treats of Cannes as the day comes to an end. Le Suquet's charming bistros provide delicious Provençal food that lets you experience the tastes of the area. Memories of a day excursion that goes beyond the ordinary and embraces the exceptional along the sun-kissed sands of the French Riviera fill the return ride to Nice with reflections on a day rich in culture, elegance, and the attraction of luxury.

Antibes

Take a fascinating day excursion from Nice to Antibes, a charming French Riviera town that offers a unique combination of culture, history, and Mediterranean charm. Take a stroll down the shore as the sun rises, illuminating Nice with a golden glow as you take in the stunning sights of the blue sea and verdant surroundings.

The striking walls around the medieval town of Antibes are the first thing that enchants visitors. Standing as motionless sentinels, these 16th-century defenses are a testament to centuries of maritime history. Explore the riches of Old

Antibes' quaint cafés, art galleries, and lovely shops as you meander along its cobblestone alleyways.

Located within the storied Château Grimaldi, the Picasso Museum is sure to be a highlight of your day. Admire the vast array of Picasso's creations, which he produced while residing in Antibes in 1946. The small-scale museum within the castle's stone walls offers a distinctive background for the artists' creations.

Take a leisurely walk down the Quai des milliardaires, a waterfront promenade dotted with opulent yachts and little seafood eateries, while the Mediterranean sunsets. Savor a leisurely meal of seafood and Provençal delicacies while taking in the laid-back vibe of this beachside sanctuary.

Discover the charms of the Cap d'Antibes in the afternoon. Here, you'll find quiet coves and immaculate beaches waiting to be discovered. The lovely seaside walk invites you to enjoy the peace of the French Riviera by providing stunning views of the Mediterranean.

Enjoy a peaceful time at the Garoupe Lighthouse as the day comes to an end. Situated on a hill, it offers expansive views of the coastline. Your day excursion will be a tapestry woven with moments of discovery, beauty, and the undeniable romance of the French Riviera, thanks to Antibes' ageless appeal and nautical tradition. Bring back with you heartfelt recollections of the magic that may be discovered a short distance from the bustling metropolis of Nice.

Eze Village

Travel from Nice to the charming medieval village of Eze Village, which is set on hillsides with a stunning view of the Mediterranean, for a magnificent day excursion. Driving down the French Riviera's meandering roads offers breathtaking vistas that hint at the splendor of Eze just as you leave the seaside charm of Nice behind.

A living picture stuck in time, Eze Village is characterized by its cobblestone streets and historic stone structures. Because of the road's views of the surrounding lush foliage and the blue sea below, the drive itself becomes an essential component of the experience.

Discover surprising discoveries at every bend of Eze's maze-like alleyways once you arrive. Those who climb will find rewards like panoramic views of the coastline and a floral garden called Jardin Exotique, high atop the cliffs.

One of the most impressive sites is the remains of Eze Castle, a legendary medieval castle. Consider the echoes of millennia past as you stroll through its stone passageways. Immerse yourself in the artistic process of creating perfumes with the unique scent of the Fragonard Perfume Factory, which adds yet another dimension to Eze's sensory experience.

Enjoy the fusion of classic Niçois food and the charms of al fresco dining at one of Eze's little eateries. The hamlet gets a lovely light over its winding alleyways as the day goes on, transformed into a painting by the warm tones of the setting sun.

After spending a day immersed in history, culture, and the enduring beauty of the French Riviera, return to Nice with a lasting recollection of Eze Village. Cherish not just the tangible mementos but also the intangible ones. Experiencing the essence of the Mediterranean character, a day excursion to Eze from Nice is more than simply a trek across space.

CONCLUSION

In concluding this Nice Travel Guide, I extend my heartfelt gratitude to you, dear reader, for choosing this companion on your journey through the sun-kissed streets of Nice. As you close the pages of this guidebook, I hope it has served as a valuable resource, unlocking the treasures of this enchanting city along the French Riviera.

Throughout these pages, we've explored the vibrant neighborhoods, historical landmarks, and cultural nuances that make Nice a captivating destination. From the sun-drenched Promenade des Anglais to the winding alleys of Vieux Nice, each corner reveals a piece of the city's rich tapestry.

Whether you're a traveler seeking adventure or a connoisseur of art, cuisine, and history, Nice offers an immersive experience that transcends the ordinary. The guide has been crafted to provide practical information, insider tips, and a glimpse into the soul of this Mediterranean gem.

As you set forth on your exploration, may the memories forged in Nice linger as cherished moments, and the insights gained enhance your travel experience. Remember the taste of traditional Niçois cuisine, the panoramic views from Castle Hill, and the timeless charm of Old Town.

Your journey doesn't end with these pages; it merely begins. Nice awaits with open arms, ready to reveal its secrets and weave unforgettable tales. Thank you for entrusting this guidebook to be your compass in the capital of the Cote d'Azur.

Wishing you a journey filled with discovery, joy, and the ineffable magic of Nice. Safe travels!

Printed in Great Britain
by Amazon

40914721R00096